2

PATHWAYS
THIRD EDITION

Listening, Speaking, and Critical Thinking

BECKY TARVER CHASE

CHRISTIEN LEE

Fil

NATIONAL GEOGRAPHIC LEARNING

Australia · Brazil · Canada · Mexico · Singapore · United Kingdom · United States

National Geographic Learning,
a Cengage Company

Pathways 2: Listening, Speaking, and Critical Thinking, 3rd Edition
Becky Tarver Chase and Christien Lee

Publisher: Sherrise Roehr

Executive Editor: Laura Le Dréan

Senior Development Editor: Lisl Bove

Director of Global Marketing: Ian Martin

Heads of Regional Marketing:

  Charlotte Ellis (Europe, Middle East and Africa)

  Justin Kaley (Asia and Greater China)

  Irina Pereyra (Latin America)

  Joy MacFarland (US and Canada)

Product Marketing Manager: Tracy Bailie

Content Project Manager: Samantha Bertschmann

Media Researcher: Leila Hishmeh

Senior Designer: Heather Marshall

Operations Support: Hayley Chwazik-Gee

Manufacturing Planner: Terry Isabella

Composition: MPS North America LLC

For permission to use material from this text or product, submit all requests online at **cengage.com/permissions**
Further permissions questions can be emailed to
permissionrequest@cengage.com

Student's Book
ISBN: 978-0-357-97892-4
Student's Book with the Spark platform:
ISBN: 978-0-357-97891-7

National Geographic Learning
5191 Natorp Blvd,
Mason, OH 45040
USA

Locate your local office at **international.cengage.com/region**

Visit National Geographic Learning online at **ELTNGL.com**
Visit our corporate website at **www.cengage.com**

Printed in China
Print Number: 01 Print Year: 2023

Scope and Sequence

* With slideshow
◆ With animation

Speaking & Pronunciation	Grammar & Vocabulary	Critical Thinking	Final Tasks
• Keep a Conversation Going • Suffixes and Syllable Stress • Participate in a Group Discussion	• Gerunds as Subjects and Objects • Meaning from Context	• Interpret Visuals	**Option 1** Play a Healthy-Habits Bingo Game **Option 2** Discuss Your Healthy Habits
• Give Reasons • Long and Short Vowels • Acknowledge Ideas and Disagree Politely	• Present Perfect • Signal Words with the Present Perfect • Collocations	• Synthesize	**Option 1** Discuss Human and Machine Intelligence **Option 2** Present a Useful App
• Define Unfamiliar Terms • The Vowel Sound /ɜr/ • Repeat and Emphasize	• Adjective Clauses • Noun and Adjective Suffixes	• Consider Different Perspectives	**Option 1** Discuss Something Popular from Another Culture **Option 2** Present Your Identity
• Give and Ask for Opinions • Spelling Patterns for Long Vowel Sounds • Participate in a Debate	• Active vs. Passive Voice • Parts of Speech	• Prioritize	**Option 1** Discuss How Grocery Stores Affect Consumers **Option 2** Debate whether Cooking Should Be Taught in Schools
• Make Suggestions • Recognize Linking • Describe Images	• Infinitives after Verbs • Words with Multiple Meanings	• Evaluate Pros and Cons	**Option 1** Discuss Strategies for Learning a Language **Option 2** Present Advice to Future Students

Scope and Sequence

* With slideshow
♦ With animation

Compelling photography and infographics in **Explore the Theme** draw students into the unit, develop their visual and information literacy skills, and get them speaking.

A **multimedia approach** featuring videos, slideshows, and animations supports listening comprehension while making content accessible and engaging.

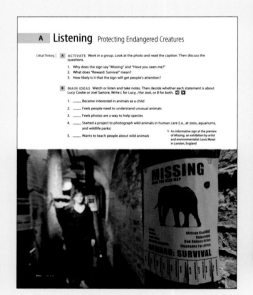

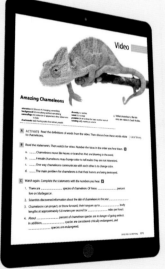

Updated Speaking Activities give more guided instruction and language support, building fluency, accuracy, and learner independence.

Academic competency skills like collaboration, communication, and problem-solving help students develop the skills and behaviors needed to succeed in school and their lives.

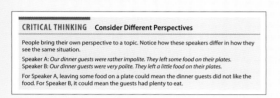

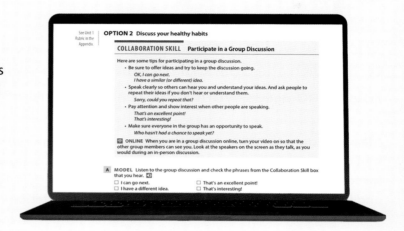

Assessment

Pathways Listening, Speaking, and Critical Thinking supports teachers and learners with various forms of assessment, with the goal of helping students achieve real-world success.

A **new Review section** provides additional opportunities for formative assessment and encourages students to take control of their learning journey through guided self-assessment.

The **Final Tasks** section with two options provides flexibility for various learning environments and another opportunity for formative assessment.

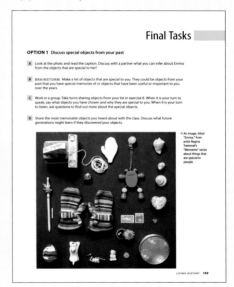

Opportunities for online assessment on the **new Spark platform** include:

- The National Geographic Learning Online Placement Test, which places students into the correct level of *Pathways*
- Interactive Online Practice activities and online tests from the Assessment Suite, for formative and summative assessment
- A Course Gradebook that tracks student and class performance against learning objectives, providing teachers with actionable insights to support student's progress

spark

Bring the world to the classroom and the classroom to life with the Spark platform — where you can prepare, teach and assess your classes all in one place!

Manage your course and teach great classes with integrated digital teaching and learning tools. Spark brings together everything you need on an all-in-one platform with a single log-in.

Track student and class performance on independent online practice and assessment. The Course Gradebook helps you turn information into insights to make the most of valuable classroom time.

Set up classes and roster students quickly and easily on Spark. Seamless integration options and point-of-use support helps you focus on what matters most: student success.

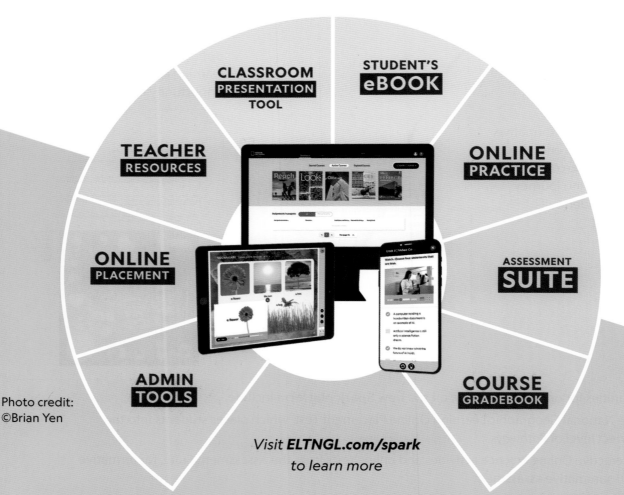

CLASSROOM PRESENTATION TOOL

STUDENT'S eBOOK

TEACHER RESOURCES

ONLINE PRACTICE

ONLINE PLACEMENT

ASSESSMENT SUITE

ADMIN TOOLS

COURSE GRADEBOOK

Photo credit:
©Brian Yen

Visit **ELTNGL.com/spark**
to learn more

HEALTHY LIVES 1

A subway train with a
healthy and happy theme
in Hangzhou, Zhejiang
province, China

IN THIS UNIT, YOU WILL:

- Watch or listen to a talk about managing stress
- Watch a video on positive stress
- Listen to a conversation about food allergies
- Play a healthy-habits bingo game
  OR Discuss your healthy habits

THINK AND DISCUSS:

1. How does the subway train encourage health and happiness?

2. Would riding on this subway train to or from work make you feel less stress?

3. What does "a healthy life" mean to you?

EXPLORE THE THEME

Look at the information. Then discuss the questions.

1. What three things add the most years to your life? What do you think the reasons are?

2. Would cyclist Robert Marchand agree with the science in the infographic?

3. What other things do you think help people to live a long life?

What Makes You Live Longer?

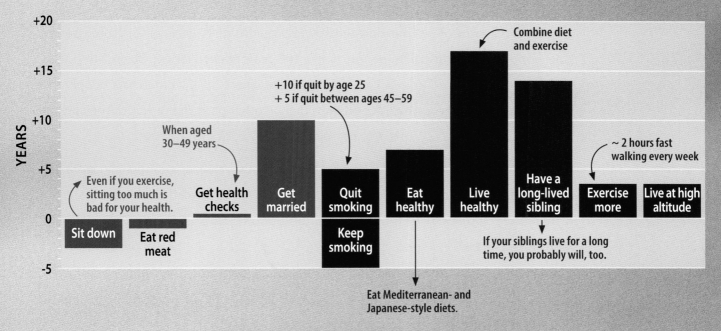

YEARS

+20
+15
+10
+5
0
-5

Combine diet and exercise

+10 if quit by age 25
+ 5 if quit between ages 45–59

When aged 30–49 years

Even if you exercise, sitting too much is bad for your health.

~ **2 hours fast walking every week**

Sit down | Eat red meat | Get health checks | Get married | Quit smoking | Eat healthy | Live healthy | Have a long-lived sibling | Exercise more | Live at high altitude

Keep smoking

If your siblings live for a long time, you probably will, too.

Eat Mediterranean- and Japanese-style diets.

STRENGTH OF SCIENCE: ■ Good ■ Strong

Source: https://informationisbeautiful.net/visualizations/what-could-really-increase-life-expectancy-lifespan-and-longevity/

At age 105, cyclist Robert Marchand tries to break the world record in the senior endurance race in Saint-Quentin-en-Yvelines, France. He said his long and active life was thanks to a diet of mainly fruits and vegetables, a little meat and coffee, and an hour of cycling a day.

A Vocabulary

A Listen and repeat. Check (✓) the words you know. 🔊

attitude (n)	**develop** (v)	**harmful** (adj)	**manage** (v)	**prevent** (v)
cause (v)	**habit** (n)	**likely** (adj)	**positive** (adj)	**provide** (v)

B **MEANING FROM CONTEXT** Listen and write the words you hear. Then think about each word's meaning. 🔊

LIVING TO 100

How old is the oldest person you know? 80 years old? 90 years old? In some parts of the world, it's not unusual for people to live 100 years or even longer. Scientists looked at two of these places—Sardinia, Italy, and Okinawa, Japan—and learned that people there ¹_____ fewer health problems than in other parts of the world. They are also more ²_____ to live to be 100 or older.

In Sardinia, scientists were surprised to find as many men as women who were 100 years old or older. This is unusual because, in general, women live longer than men. One reason for this may be that men in Sardinia don't have a lot of stress in their lives, and stress can be ³_____. It can ⁴_____ health problems. The men there work outdoors, which ⁵_____ daily exercise, while the women ⁶_____ the house and money. According to one Sardinian man, he does the work, but his wife does the worrying.

In Okinawa, people have very little cancer and heart disease. One of the reasons could be their ⁷_____ ⁸_____ toward life. That might ⁹_____ stress. In addition, Okinawans eat a healthy diet that includes a lot of fresh vegetables and a little meat and fish. They also have healthy ¹⁰_____, such as taking care of a garden and spending time with family. In other words, a positive attitude and good food seem to prevent many of the health problems found in other parts of the world.

A man from Sardinia, Italy ▶

C Write each word from exercise A next to its definition.

1. _____ (v) to control or deal with something

2. _____ (v) to start to have

3. _____ (adj) possible or probable

4. _____ (v) to make something happen

5. _____ (adj) causing negative effects or damage

6. _____ (v) to give something or make it available

7. _____ (v) to stop something from happening

8. _____ (n) something you do often and regularly

9. _____ (n) a feeling about someone or something

10. _____ (adj) good or helpful

D Complete the sentences with the correct form of a word from exercise C.

1. In Okinawa, good food and healthy _____ may _____ health problems.

2. My father always thinks he's going to get sick, but I have a better _____. I tell myself I'm going to stay healthy!

3. My grandmother is 90 and very healthy. I think she is _____ to live to be 100.

4. Stella made several _____ changes to her diet and she feels great!

5. Using the calendar app on my phone helps me to _____ my schedule.

6. When the weather changes, many people _____ colds.

7. Eating too much fried food can _____ health problems.

8. Some schools _____ free lunch to all students.

9. The sugar in candy can be _____ to your teeth. Don't eat too much of it.

E **PERSONALIZE** Check Yes or No for each question. Take turns asking and answering the questions with a partner. Explain your answers.

QUESTIONNAIRE: How likely are you to live to be 100?*

	YES	NO
1. Do you manage stress well?	☐	☐
2. Does your diet include a lot of fruits and vegetables?	☐	☐
3. Do you exercise for 30 minutes a day or more?	☐	☐
4. Is anyone in your family 90 or older?	☐	☐
5. In general, do you have a positive attitude toward life?	☐	☐

*The more questions you answered with yes, the more likely you are to live to be 100.

A Listening How to Manage Stress

Critical Thinking **A** **PREDICT** You will hear a talk about stress and how to manage it. Discuss these questions.

1. What is stress? What causes it? What do you do to manage stress?

2. How do you think the speaker will organize the talk?
   a. Explain what stress is and then talk about one way to manage it
   b. Talk about ways to manage stress and then explain what it is
   c. Explain what stress is and then talk about different ways to manage it

3. Which topics do you expect to hear about in the talk?
   a. diet   c. sleep   e. social life
   b. exercise   d. smoking   f. taking breaks

LISTENING SKILL   Listen for Main Ideas and Details

When listening to a talk, you need to be able to identify the main ideas and details.

Main ideas are the speaker's most important ideas. Here are some techniques to help you identify main ideas:

- Listen carefully to the beginning of a talk. Most speakers will mention the main ideas in their introduction.
- Listen for repetition. Speakers often repeat key words and phrases or use synonyms to emphasize their main ideas.

Details give more information about the main ideas. They include facts, examples, reasons, stories, and other information that makes the main ideas clearer and more interesting.

Another country with very healthy people is Switzerland. ***Many people there live to be 84 years old. Reasons for this might be their busy lives and the clean mountain air.***

B **MAIN IDEAS** Read the statements from the talk. Then watch or listen to the talk and complete each statement with the words you hear. 🔊 ▶

1. Tonight, I'm going to talk with you about _____ and how to _____ it.

2. . . . let's think about what _____ and also about the way _____.

3. Another important topic is the _____. It certainly can be harmful to our health.

4. On the other hand, _____, too.

Being by blue spaces (the sea, rivers, lakes, etc.) is good for people's mental health.

C DETAILS Listen again. Complete the notes on the talk with the details from the box. Write one letter for each detail. 🔊

Stress	How to Manage Stress

• Causes of stress
   Detail: [1]_____
	• Get enough exercise
	   Detail: [5]_____

• Feelings of stress Detail: [2]_____	• Get enough sleep; be social; try yoga or music

• Effects of stress
   ○ Harmful effects
      Detail: [3]_____
   ○ Helpful effects
      Detail: [4]_____
	• Have a positive attitude about stress
	   Detail: [6]_____

a. heart beats faster; breathing changes; headache or stomach problems
b. walk, run, or play a sport at least four or five days a week
c. high blood pressure or other health problems
d. extra energy to do difficult or challenging things
e. think of stress as something that can be helpful
f. busy lives, including schoolwork, jobs, and raising children

D FOCUSED LISTENING Listen to an excerpt from the talk and write the words you hear. What important idea is the speaker emphasizing? 🔊

I'm Tara Sorenson, and I'm a public [1]_____ nurse. Public [2]_____

nurses are like other nurses, but we take care of more than one person. Our job is to keep

everyone in the community [3]_____. [. . .] I hope to provide information that will

help all of you to live longer, [4]_____ lives.

A Speaking

See Verbs
Followed by
Gerunds or
Infinitives in
the Appendix.

Critical Thinking | **A** **APPLY** Listening A was a talk by a public health nurse about stress and how to manage it. Read the information below. Then discuss the questions with a partner.

> Public health nurses are different from nurses who work in a hospital or doctor's office. They often work for the government or other groups that help communities. Their job is to keep communities healthy and safe. A big part of their job is educating people about health topics.

1. Where do you think a public health nurse might give this kind of talk? (e.g., at a company, at a university, at a public library, etc.)
2. What is the easiest kind of health advice to follow? The hardest?
3. What advice might you give a friend about managing stress?

GRAMMAR FOR SPEAKING Gerunds as Subjects and Objects

A *gerund* is the base verb plus *-ing*. Gerunds act as nouns. We often use them as the subjects of sentences. A gerund subject is always singular.

> ***Walking*** *is my favorite kind of exercise.*
> ***Listening*** *to music is a great way to relax.*

We also use gerunds as the object of certain verbs or the object of prepositions.

> *My doctor* <u>recommends</u> ***sleeping*** *seven or more hours every night.*
> *Now I want to learn more* <u>about</u> ***managing*** *stress.*

Verbs that are often followed by a gerund object include:

admit	consider	dislike	finish	(don't) mind	postpone	suggest
avoid	discuss	enjoy	keep	miss	recommend	

B Write the gerund form of the verb in parentheses. Then choose S if the gerund is the *subject* of the sentence, OV if it's the *object of a verb*, or OP if it's the *object of a preposition*.

1. _____ (sleep) for eight hours a night is a good goal.   S   OV   OP

2. My sister is afraid of _____ (hurt) her knees, so she won't exercise with me.   S   OV   OP

3. My grandmother suggests _____ (walk) for 30 minutes every morning.   S   OV   OP

4. She enjoys _____ (see) her friends in the park.   S   OV   OP

5. Jamal is excited about _____ (lose) three kilos last month.   S   OV   OP

6. _____ (learn) to relax is important—even for young children.   S   OV   OP

C Interview a partner using the questions. Then make your own questions using expressions from the box below. Practice using gerunds.

1. What do you enjoy doing in your free time?
2. What do you avoid doing because you don't like doing it?
3. What is something you did as a child that you miss doing now?
4. What are some things you are considering doing in the future?

dislike eating	suggest watching	finish reading	keep practicing

D **EVALUATE** Work with a partner. Look at the photo and read the information about Dr. Levine's treadmill desks. Then discuss the questions that follow.

Critical Thinking

Dr. James Levine of the Mayo Clinic says that most people do far too much sitting. He created the treadmill desk so that more people can exercise while they work. In this photo, Dean of Students Sue Porter of The Branson School in Ross, California, USA, talks to students while using her treadmill desk in her office.

1. How often do you take a break and move around when you are studying or working at a computer?
2. Do you think a treadmill desk is a good idea? How about a standing desk? Explain.
3. A treadmill desk is an unusual way to exercise. What are some other unusual ways to exercise?

PRONUNCIATION Suffixes and Syllable Stress

🔊 When the suffixes *-(t)ion, -ity, -ic,* and *-ical* are added to words, the stressed syllable can change. The syllable just before each of these suffixes receives the main or primary stress.

-(t)ion (noun ending)
e•du•cate—e•du•ca•tion

-ity (noun ending)
pro•ba•ble—pro•ba•bi•li•ty

-ic (adjective ending)
sci•ence—sci•en•ti•fic

-ical (adjective ending)
hi•sto•ry—hi•stor•i•cal

E Underline the syllable that gets the main stress in each word. Listen to check your answers. Then practice saying the words. 🔊

1. va•<u>ca</u>•tion
2. ba•sic
3. i•den•ti•ty
4. me•di•cal
5. spe•ci•fic
6. ques•tion

7. u•ni•ver•si•ty
8. mu•si•cal
9. di•rec•tion
10. e•lec•tro•nic
11. ac•ti•vi•ty
12. ty•pi•cal

F Say the words in the box with a partner. Then complete the sentences with the words.

availability	information	presidential
economical	location	technological

1. The nurse was well informed. He gave me good _____.

2. Yoga classes sound good, but I don't know about their _____ in my city.

3. Anna knows a lot about technology, and we have a _____ problem. Let's ask her!

4. She is not the company president, but her blue suit looks _____, I think.

5. I can't find the gym on this map. Do you know the _____?

6. I like eating at restaurants, but eating at home is more _____.

Critical Thinking | **G** **APPLY** High school can cause a lot of stress for teenagers. With a small group, make a list of things that can stress teens out. Then discuss how communication, preparation, and different forms of relaxation could help teens manage their stress.

Video

Positive Stress

simulator (n) a machine that helps people learn to fly
setback (n) a problem that stops or slows your progress

slip away (v phr) to slowly disappear
master (v) to gain complete knowledge or skill

▲ A flight instructor and a trainee pilot in a simulator

A Match each word from the video with its definition. Use a dictionary if needed.

1. _____ captain
2. _____ challenging
3. _____ confidence
4. _____ disappointment
5. _____ excitement
6. _____ face
7. _____ overcome
8. _____ satisfaction

a. a feeling of belief in your abilities
b. the person in charge of an airplane
c. a feeling of sadness about the results of something
d. a feeling of happiness about the results of something
e. a feeling of happiness about something to come
f. difficult
g. to see that there is a problem and try to deal with it
h. to succeed in dealing with something difficult

B Watch the video. Complete the summary with words you hear. ▶

Iris de Kan wants to become the ¹_____ of an airplane. The training is quite ²_____, and she spends a lot of time practicing. Her first task is a ³_____ in a simulator. She doesn't ⁴_____ the test at first, but she doesn't let her ⁵_____ stop her. She continues with the training, works hard, and masters ⁶_____. Positive stress, or eustress, helped her achieve her goal.

C **PERSONALIZE** Work with a small group. Discuss a time when stress has helped you accomplish a goal.

B Vocabulary

Listen and repeat. Check the words you know. 🔊

attach (v)	**common** (adj)	**defend** (v)	**reaction** (n)	**substance** (n)
avoid (v)	**contain** (v)	**produce** (v)	**research** (n)	**theory** (n)

MEANING FROM CONTEXT Listen and write the words you hear. 🔊

ALLERGIES

Definition: If you have an *allergy* to something, you become sick, or have an allergic [1]_____, when you eat it, touch it, or breathe it in. These allergic reactions can be serious, so people who had allergic reactions in the past need to [2]_____ the [3]_____ they are allergic to.

Process: After someone eats, touches, or breathes in something they are allergic to, their bodies [4]_____ antibodies.[1] These antibodies [5]_____ to cells that usually [6]_____ the body against health problems. But in people with allergies, these cells produce substances that cause allergic reactions such as sneezing, itching, and breathing problems.

Common Allergens (things that cause allergies):

1. Food: Milk, eggs, soy, and peanuts can cause problems, and so can foods that [7]_____ these ingredients.

2. Pollen: Plant allergies are often seasonal (more [8]_____ in the spring and summer).

3. Insect bites: Stings from bees and wasps are dangerous for people with allergies.

Causes: There are many causes of allergies. For example, if your parents have allergies, you are more likely to have them, too. The stress of modern life could be another cause. Surprisingly, living in an environment that is too clean could also cause allergies! One [9]_____ is that dirt is good for us. [10]_____ shows that allergies are not common among people who live with farm animals.

[1]**antibodies** (n): substances your body produces to fight disease

12 UNIT 1 LESSON B

C Write each word from exercise A next to its definition.

1. _____ (n) a certain kind of material

2. _____ (v) to join or connect to something

3. _____ (v) to make or create

4. _____ (n) an action or change (often negative) in response to something

5. _____ (v) to protect

6. _____ (v) to stay away from something

7. _____ (v) to have something inside

8. _____ (adj) usual

9. _____ (n) work that involves studying something

10. _____ (n) an idea used to explain something

VOCABULARY SKILL   Meaning from Context

It's often possible to guess the meaning of a new word by paying attention to the information around it, or the context. For example, look at this sentence:

*These cells produce substances that cause allergic **reactions** such as sneezing, itching, and breathing problems.*

Even if you don't know what **reaction** means, you know that sneezing, itching, and breathing problems are responses to something. Other common kinds of context clues are antonyms or contrasts (*common/unusual*), definitions or restatements (*reactions— negative responses to something*), and synonyms (*big/large*).

D Underline the words and phrases that help you understand the words in **bold**.

1. My seasonal allergies are very **mild**; on the other hand, I am extremely allergic to bee stings.

2. Knowing what food allergies you have is important so you can avoid the **culprits**—the specific things that give you problems.

3. In the spring and summer months, Jenny **suffers** from hay fever. She feels ill, as if she has a bad cold or flu.

4. Simon is allergic to **dairy**, so he can't eat cheese, yogurt, or anything made with milk.

E **PERSONALIZE** Work with a partner. Discuss the questions.

1. What foods do you or someone you know **avoid** eating? Why?

2. What do you think of the **theory** that living in an environment that is too clean could cause allergies?

B Listening Living with Food Allergies

Critical Thinking **A** **ACTIVATE** You are going to hear a conversation between two students. One of the students has food allergies. Discuss these questions with a group.

1. A term for speaking up and asking for what you need is "self-advocacy." How do you think people with food allergies might *advocate* for themselves, or explain their situation, when they eat at a school cafeteria? When they eat at a friend's house?

2. When you want or need something specific, how do you feel about asking for it? For example, if you cannot hear a teacher who is speaking softly, what do you do?

NOTE-TAKING SKILL   Take Effective Notes

Taking notes while you listen can be very helpful if you follow a few guidelines.

Listen for the right things

Focus on main ideas and important details. Details are important if they provide reasons, examples, or other information that make the main ideas clearer.

It's not possible or necessary to write every word you hear. Focus on key words, not complete sentences, and use abbreviations (short forms) and symbols.

Organize your notes

Organize your notes to show the relationships between ideas. A graphic organizer such as a T-chart or time line can be helpful.

Review and rewrite your notes

Soon after you take notes, read them and add to or clarify the information—before you forget what you heard. That way your notes will make sense and be useful to you.

B **MAIN IDEAS** Listen to the conversation and decide what the people mainly talk about. 🔊

a. How Elena feels about having food allergies
b. Elena's allergies and how she takes care of herself
c. School policies that help people with food allergies

C **DETAILS** Listen again and complete the notes. 🔊

Elena's allergies	How Elena advocates for herself
• 1_____ • 2_____ • 3_____	• Before she goes to someone's house, she 4_____ or 5_____ a message to explain her food allergies. • At school, she 6_____ to the cafeteria workers and 7_____ about ingredients in dishes.

D Listen to an excerpt from the conversation. Discuss what you think Elena means.

CRITICAL THINKING   Interpret Visuals

Visuals, such as graphs, maps, charts, and infographics, are used to show information in a clear way. To analyze a visual, first look at the title. Then look at how the data is displayed. Some visuals will contain a key that explains what different colors, symbols, and other elements mean. Think about the main point that the visual is trying to make, as well as questions you have about the data presented.

E Look at the infographic and discuss the questions with a partner. Critical Thinking

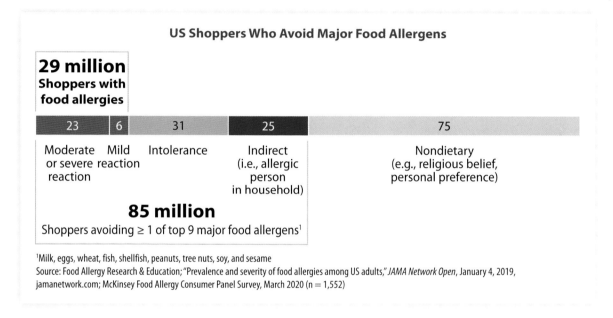

US Shoppers Who Avoid Major Food Allergens

29 million
Shoppers with food allergies

23	6	31	25	75
Moderate or severe reaction	Mild reaction	Intolerance	Indirect (i.e., allergic person in household)	Nondietary (e.g., religious belief, personal preference)

85 million
Shoppers avoiding ≥ 1 of top 9 major food allergens[1]

[1]Milk, eggs, wheat, fish, shellfish, peanuts, tree nuts, soy, and sesame
Source: Food Allergy Research & Education; "Prevalence and severity of food allergies among US adults," *JAMA Network Open*, January 4, 2019, jamanetwork.com; McKinsey Food Allergy Consumer Panel Survey, March 2020 (n = 1,552)

1. What country is the information from?
2. What group of people is the information about?
3. What are the reasons for this behavior?
4. What is the main point of the infographic?
5. What questions do you have about the main point or data?

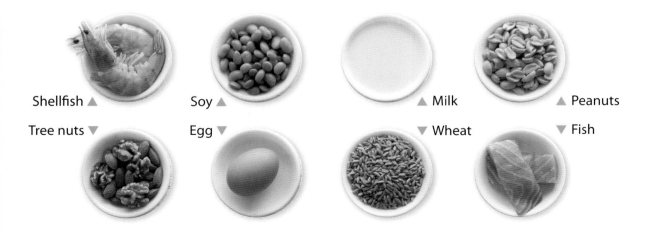

Shellfish ▲   Soy ▲   ▲ Milk   ▲ Peanuts

Tree nuts ▼   Egg ▼   ▼ Wheat   ▼ Fish

B Speaking

Critical Thinking

A **EXPLAIN** Listening B was a conversation about living with allergies. Work with a group. Discuss the questions.

1. The speakers from the conversation mentioned a campus food policy. Do you think it's important for schools and offices to have policies like this? Explain.
2. Do you think this information about food allergies will affect your life? For example, will you think or do anything differently?

Critical Thinking

B **EVALUATE** Some scientists are working to genetically modify foods to remove the things that cause allergies. Discuss the questions.

1. How is genetically modifying foods to make them less allergenic a good idea? A bad idea?
2. If soybeans were genetically modified to remove allergens, what foods could people with soybean allergies eat?
3. Would you eat genetically modified food that was made less allergenic? Why or why not?

See Speaking Phrases in the Appendix.

SPEAKING SKILL   Keep a Conversation Going

Keeping a conversation going is considered polite and is an important communication skill. Here are some ways to do it.

Show the speaker that you are listening and are interested in what they are saying. Look at her, nod your head, and comment on what she says.

> A: *I'm going to Australia this summer.*
> B: *Oh, really? That's wonderful!*

Ask a follow-up question. Avoid *yes/no* questions. Use *wh-* questions instead. *Wh-* questions require speakers to give more information in their answers.

> *What are you going to do there?*
> *How's the weather there in July?*
> *Which cities are you visiting?*

C Listen to the short conversations. Check (✓) the way each speaker keeps the conversation going. 🔊

	Shows interest	**Asks a follow-up question**
1.	☐	☐
2.	☐	☐
3.	☐	☐
4.	☐	☐

D With a partner, take turns suggesting topics from the box below, or use your own ideas. Practice keeping the conversation going by showing interest and asking follow-up questions.

| friends | interesting places/travel | ways to relax | sports |
| exercise | healthy food | jobs/careers | phone apps |

A: *Let's talk about interesting places.*
B: *OK. What interesting places have you visited?*
A: *Well, I went to Costa Rica with my sister last summer. It was amazing!*
B: *Really? What did you do there?*

E **PERSONALIZE** Work with your partner. Which of these health topics are the most important to you? Why?

Living a long life   Managing stress
Eating a healthy diet   Living with allergies
Getting enough exercise   Being your own health advocate

▼ Studies show that looking at calm pictures of nature can help you relax.

Review

SELF-ASSESS

How well can you . . . ?	Very well.	OK.	I need improvement.
use the key vocabulary	☐	☐	☐
say words with suffixes -(t)ion, -ity, -ic, -ical	☐	☐	☐
keep a conversation going	☐	☐	☐
use gerunds as subjects and objects	☐	☐	☐

A VOCABULARY   Check the words you can use. Then complete the tasks.

attach (v)	common (adj)	habit (n)	positive (adj)	reaction (n)
attitude (n)	contain (v)	harmful (adj)	prevent (v)	research (n)
avoid (v)	defend (v)	likely (adj)	produce (v)	substance (n)
cause (v)	develop (v)	manage (v)	provide (v)	theory (n)

1. Look up any words you didn't check. Then write a sentence or question with the word.

2. Complete the questions about health.

   a. We can't always prevent stress, so what are some good ways to _____ it?

   b. What are some things we should avoid because they are _____ to our health?

B PRONUNCIATION   Underline the stressed syllable in each word.

1. a•ller•gic
2. the••o•re•ti•cal
3. e•lec•tri•ci•ty
4. lo•ca•tion
5. pro•duc•tion
6. po•si•ti•vi•ty

C GRAMMAR   Complete each sentence with a gerund.

1. _____ healthy food can help you live longer.

2. After school I usually relax by _____.

3. _____ is a type of exercise I really enjoy.

D SPEAKING SKILL   Write responses to keep the conversation going.

1. A: I made a really delicious salad yesterday.

   B: _____

2. A: I took a great trip last year.

   B: _____

RE-ASSESS   What skills or language still need improvement?

Final Tasks

OPTION 1 Play a healthy-habits bingo game

A Look at the bingo card below. As your teacher calls out the squares, draw an "X" over every healthy habit that you have. Everyone can mark the Free Space. The winner is the first person to mark all the squares in a row, column, or diagonally across the board.

	B	I	N	G	O
1	eat a healthy breakfast	play a sport	go for walks	go to bed at the same time each night	spend time relaxing
2	talk with friends and family on the phone	laugh at something funny	avoid eating unhealthy foods	stretch or do yoga	have regular health appointments
3	have a positive attitude about life	sleep for >7 hours each night	**Free Space**	spend time with friends and family	drink plenty of water
4	avoid "screen time" for an hour before bed	eat plenty of fruits and vegetables	spend time on my hobby	exercise several times per week	recognize when stress is helpful
5	write in a journal	ask for help when I need it	read books	take deep breaths to be calm	listen to music

B Work in a small group. Take turns giving details about some of your healthy habits. Show interest in what each person is saying and ask some follow-up questions.

▼ A family plays bingo after dinner.

OPTION 2 Discuss your healthy habits

COLLABORATION SKILL   Participate in a Group Discussion

Here are some tips for participating in a group discussion.

- Be sure to offer ideas and try to keep the discussion going.

    OK, I can go next.
    I have a similar (or different) idea.

- Speak clearly so others can hear you and understand your ideas. And ask people to repeat their ideas if you don't hear or understand them.

    Sorry, could you repeat that?

- Pay attention and show interest when other people are speaking.

    That's an excellent point!
    That's interesting!

- Make sure everyone in the group has an opportunity to speak.

    Who hasn't had a chance to speak yet?

📶 **ONLINE** When you are in a group discussion online, turn your video on so that the other group members can see you. Look at the speakers on the screen as they talk, as you would during an in-person discussion.

A MODEL Listen to the group discussion and check the phrases from the Collaboration Skill box that you hear. 🔊

☐ I can go next.   ☐ That's an excellent point!
☐ I have a different idea.   ☐ That's interesting!
☐ Sorry, could you repeat that?   ☐ Who hasn't had the chance to speak yet?

B ANALYZE THE MODEL Listen again and check the categories you hear the speakers talk about. 🔊

☐ diet   ☐ sleep
☐ exercise habits   ☐ social life
☐ mental health habits

C PLAN On a separate piece of paper, take notes on your healthy habits. Think about the categories in exercise B. How do those things make you healthier?

D DISCUSS Work in a small group. Use your notes from exercise C to discuss your healthy habits and how they make you healthier. Make sure everyone participates and asks group members follow-up questions.

TECHNOLOGY TODAY AND TOMORROW 2

Shunsuke Aoki, the CEO of Yukai Engineering in Tokyo, Japan, hugs a catlike robot created by his company.

IN THIS UNIT, YOU WILL:

- Watch or listen to a radio show about artificial intelligence
- Watch a video about underwater robots
- Listen to a conversation about tech for good
- Discuss human and machine intelligence
  OR Present a useful app

THINK AND DISCUSS:

Yukai Engineering develops personal robots to bring happiness to people's lives. The CEO believes that every home will have a social robot in the future.

1. Do you think social robots will become common?
2. Would you be interested in a social robot?

Look at the information. Then discuss the questions.

1. What are the benefits of a "smart home"?
2. What problems could a smart home have?
3. What things in your home would you like to be able to control from anywhere?

The Internet of Things

The Internet of Things, or IoT, is the connection that everyday objects have to each other through the Internet. Examples of IoT are smartphones, wearable technology, and smart home appliances.

One branch of IoT is smart homes. In a smart home, people can control things like lights, the temperature, and security cameras. Their digital assistant can let them know when they have almost no coffee left and then have the coffee delivered the next day.

How many things in your life are connected to the Internet?

A smart home in southern Spain

A Vocabulary

A Listen and repeat. Check the words you know. 🔊

affect (v)	**command** (n)	**data** (n)	**privacy** (n)	**reliable** (adj)
capable of (adj phr)	**concern** (n)	**pattern** (n)	**reduce** (v)	**trend** (n)

B **MEANING FROM CONTEXT** Listen and write the words you hear. Then think about each word's meaning. 🔊

TIME LINE OF ARTIFICIAL INTELLIGENCE (AI) HISTORY

1950

1950: In *I, Robot*, a book by Isaac Asimov, the makers of robots give the robots a [1]_____ not to harm humans.

1960

1950s: Computers become an important tool for doing calculations quickly and are more [2]_____ than humans.

1970

1960s: An industrial robot called Unimate begins to replace human workers in automobile manufacturing. It starts a global [3]_____.

1980

1990

1997: The computer Deep Blue wins a match against a world chess champion because it could process information quickly. Deep Blue's abilities [4]_____ all technology and helped start the age of big [5]_____.

2000

2011: Siri, a digital assistant, is part of the newest Apple iPhone. Siri learns from its users' [6]_____ of behavior and presents its users with the most useful data for them.

2010

2021: Universities in the USA and China show that AI can recognize a type of cancer and could [7]_____ the workload of busy doctors.

2020

2022: UNESCO publishes "Recommendation on the Ethics of AI." The document outlines ten [8]_____ about AI, including [9]_____, safety, and fairness.

2030

2022: OpenAI launches ChatGPT, a program that's [10]_____ natural language processing tasks such as text generation and language translation. As more data is collected, ChatGPT gets more precise, or accurate.

C Complete each question with a word from the box. Use each word only once. Then work with a partner to ask and answer the questions.

| capable of | concern | reduce | reliable | trend |

1. Are computers usually _____, or do they sometimes not work?

2. What are some things that most computers are _____ doing?

3. What is a popular _____ in fashion right now?

4. What is one _____ you have about the future?

5. How can people _____ the amount of time they spend on their phones?

D Match each word with its definition.

1. _____ affect   a. an order to do something

2. _____ command   b. information that is used or stored on a computer

3. _____ data   c. something that repeats in a way you can guess

4. _____ pattern   d. to cause someone or something to change

5. _____ privacy   e. the state of being free from public attention

VOCABULARY SKILL   Collocations

Collocations are words that are frequently used together. Two common types of collocations are *adjective + preposition* and *noun + preposition*.

Adjective + preposition   *Some machines are **capable of** making decisions.*
Noun + preposition   *Workers may have **concerns about** robots in the workplace.*

Knowing which words to collocate with each other will help you use new words correctly and make your English sound more fluent.

E   **EXPLAIN**   Underline the collocations. Then discuss the questions with a partner.   Critical Thinking

1. What is one thing you are afraid of?

2. What is something new that you are interested in doing?

3. What is something you would like to be famous for?

4. From the time line, can you draw conclusions about AI?

5. What type of technology are you likely to buy soon?

6. What is a pattern of behavior you notice online?

7. What technologies did ancient Egyptians have access to?

A Listening Artificial Intelligence

Critical Thinking

A **ACTIVATE** Discuss these questions with a partner.

1. What AI do you use? What works well? What problems do you have?
2. How do you feel about AI? Do you have any concerns?
3. What do you hope AI will be able to do in the future (e.g., drive a car, know how we're feeling, etc.)?

NOTE-TAKING SKILL **Write Key Words and Phrases**

When you take notes, don't try to write full sentences. Listen carefully to understand the main ideas. Then write key words and phrases that will help you remember those ideas.

You hear: *When we search the Internet, the <u>results</u> that we see are <u>chosen</u> carefully. The browser has learned which websites are the most <u>popular</u> or most <u>reliable</u>, as well as which <u>websites we visit the most</u>.*

You write: search results: most popular, reliable, visited websites

---

B **MAIN IDEAS** Watch or listen to the radio show and complete the notes with ONE word you hear. 🔊 ▶

Artificial intelligence
Two kinds of AI:

1st weak AI: does one [1]_____

2nd strong AI: has [2]_____ and does tasks on its own

How weak AI works:

Uses [3]_____ to find patterns

Finds patterns in spoken and written [4]_____

[5]_____ in AI:

In medicine: [6]_____ can recognize cancer

In [7]_____ AI = more customized and personal

Concerns about AI:

[8]_____ is a concern; our personal data is collected online

C **DETAILS** Listen again and write T for *True* or F for *False*. 🔊

1. _____ Some types of weak AI can recommend movies to watch.

2. _____ Everyone agrees that we will achieve strong AI in the future.

3. _____ AI prevents us from seeing some websites when we search the Internet.

4. _____ Digital assistants do not find patterns in data.

5. _____ Students can get support from AI in online learning programs.

6. _____ Companies can use our personal data to customize our service.

D FOCUSED LISTENING Listen and complete the sentences with ONE or TWO words. These words describe the underlined words or phrases. 🔊

1. <u>Digital assistants</u>, _____, are another great example of weak AI.

2. Another way AI works is by _____ in spoken and written language. This is called _speech recognition_.

3. They <u>customize</u> learning and make the education experience more _____.

E PERSONALIZE Work with a partner to discuss the questions.

1. Have you ever had autocorrect write a word you did not intend? Explain what happened.
2. What personal data about you do you think companies have collected online?
3. What questions do you still have about AI?

Mary Quinn is legally blind and relies on accessibility technology like her Alexa app, which is a digital assistant.

Speaking

See Past
Participles
of Irregular
Verbs in the
Appendix.

GRAMMAR FOR SPEAKING   Present Perfect

We use the present perfect to talk about:

1. Actions or situations that began in the past and continue until now.

    *My professor **has done** a lot of work in IT. (She still works in IT.)*

2. Actions or situations that have happened one or more times in the past and relate to the present. The exact time is not stated or important.

    *Leona **has taken** several courses in computer programming.*

    *We **have** never **gone** to a technology conference, so we want to go to one.*

We form the present perfect with ***have/has*** plus the past participle of a verb. We often use contractions with the present perfect.

*I**'ve learned** a lot about artificial intelligence.*

*My classmate**'s built** his own website, but he **hasn't published** it yet.*

***Have** you **used** a robot?*

A Listen to the sentences and write the words you hear. 🔊

1. I _____ customer service three times today.

2. This _____ my favorite class this semester.

3. Engineers _____ all the problems with self-driving cars.

4. Voice recognition software _____ quite good in recent years.

5. My brother _____ any other languages.

B Complete each statement with the present perfect form of the verb in parentheses. Then compare your sentences with a partner.

1. My brother _____ (call) me five times today.

2. In many fields, robots _____ (not, replace) human workers.

3. Medical researchers _____ (use) data from all over the world.

4. Understanding spoken language _____ (be) a challenge for artificial intelligence.

5. Haruki _____ (not, learn) how to program computers.

6. I _____ (take) many online classes, but I prefer in-person ones.

7. There _____ (be) many advances in wearable technology recently.

8. My parents _____ (have) a hard time keeping up with technology trends.

GRAMMAR FOR SPEAKING Signal Words with the Present Perfect

See Signal Words with the Present Perfect in the Appendix.

Signal words and phrases with the present perfect give extra information about when something happened.

For signals how long something has been true.

> We **have known** about the problem **for** over a year.

Since signals when a situation began.

> I've **had** my phone **since** last year.

Here are other signal words and phrases that are commonly used with the present perfect.

already	ever	so far	(not) yet
always	never	up to now	

> We're a new IT company, but we **have already grown** a lot.
> We **have earned** profits totaling $71,000 **so far** this year. (We might still earn more.)
> **Have** you **ever eaten** at that restaurant?

C Write the present perfect of the words in parentheses and choose the correct signal words.

1. Richard _____ (be) a videogame designer **for / since** 2019.

2. I _____ (know) him **for / since** almost ten years.

3. _____ Elena **ever / yet** _____ (visit) her cousins in Hungary?

4. No, she _____ **never / so far** _____ (be) there, unfortunately.

5. I _____ **already / up to now** _____ (finish) the homework for next Monday.

D Work with a partner. Add other actions and experiences to the list. Then ask your classmates questions with the present perfect.

A: Have you ever lost your phone?
B: No, I haven't. Have you ever lost yours?

- travel to another country
- have a part-time job
- sing in front of an audience
- read a book in another language
- arrive late for class
- give someone an expensive gift

- _____
- _____
- _____

PRONUNCIATION   Long and Short Vowels

🔊 When we pronounce short vowels, our mouth and face muscles are more relaxed, and we say the vowel sounds quickly: *miss, less, book, cup*. With long vowel sounds, our muscles are more tense, and the vowels take slightly longer to say: *phone, fine, like, place*.

short vowel	long vowel
sit	seat
mad	made
let	late
not	note
quit	quite

Spelling is sometimes helpful. Words that end with a silent *-e* (*like, same*) often have long vowel sounds. One-syllable words that end in a vowel (*see, go*) often have long vowel sounds. But words spelled with C-V-C (consonant-vowel-consonant, like *cat, him*) and C-V-C-C (consonant-vowel-consonant-consonant, like *miss, task*) often have short vowel sounds.

E Listen and choose the words you hear. 🔊

1. a. bit   b. bite
2. a. pet   b. Pete
3. a. get   b. gate
4. a. rob   b. robe
5. a. can   b. cane
6. a. loss   b. loose

F Work with a partner. Choose one of the words for each question. Ask your partner the questions. Your partner will choose the best answers.

1. Did you see the (knot / note)?
   a. No, is the necklace really tangled?
   b. Yes, I saw it posted on the classroom door.

2. How is the (car / care)?
   a. It's okay. It needs new tires.
   b. It's great! All the doctors are friendly.

3. Where is the (plan / plane)?
   a. I think it is on the desk.
   b. I think it is landing at the airport.

4. Is this the (cod / code)?
   a. Yes, I'm going to cook it for dinner.
   b. Yes, you can use it to log on to the computer.

5. Did you buy a (kit / kite)?
   a. No, I bought the toy already made.
   b. Yes, I want to fly it this afternoon.

6. Did she (fall / fail)?
   a. Yes, and she hurt her knee.
   b. No, she got an A in the course!

7. Is this (set / seat) available?
   a. No, someone already bought it.
   b. No, someone is sitting there.

Robots of the Deep

boundary (n) a limit
advancement (n) development or improvement
algorithm (n) a set of instructions for how to solve a problem or do a calculation

limitation (n) an inability that holds you back
extend one's reach (v phr) to increase one's limits
curiosity (n) a desire to know or learn something

▲ Antonella Wilby working on one of her underwater robots

A Watch the video. Complete the summary with the words in the box. ONE word is extra. ▶

3-D	curious	dive	explore
advantages	dangerous	environments	generation

National Geographic Explorer Antonella Wilby builds robots to ¹_____

ocean ²_____. Robots have ³_____ over human divers. They can go

deeper under water, stay under water for a longer time, and go into more ⁴_____

places than humans can. The robots Antonella works on have cameras for eyes. She uses

the ⁵_____ information they collect to create maps. She is working on the next

⁶_____ of robots. These new robots will be ⁷_____ and know what

they should take pictures of without humans telling them.

B Watch again. Write T for *True* and F for *False*. ▶

1. _____ Antonella likes problems that she needs science and technology to solve.

2. _____ The robots' cameras work differently from people's eyes.

3. _____ Robots aren't very good at doing what humans tell them to.

4. _____ Robots can help humans overcome their limitations under water.

C **ANALYZE** Work with a partner. Discuss some advantages and disadvantages of robots being curious.

Critical Thinking

B Vocabulary

A Listen and repeat. Check the words you know. 🔊

collaboration (n)	**develop** (v)	**inspire** (v)	**inventor** (n)	**turn into** (v phr)
contribute (v)	**device** (n)	**invention** (n)	**lead** (v)	**work on** (v phr)

B **MEANING FROM CONTEXT** Listen and write the words you hear. Then think about each word's meaning. 🔊

NATIONAL GEOGRAPHIC YOUNG EXPLORER GITANJALI RAO

When you hear the word [1]"_____," what kind of person comes to mind—male or female? Young, middle-aged, or older? Someone who [2]_____ or someone who follows? Of course, the person has probably had an idea they [3]_____ something new, but what else does the word mean?

Gitanjali Rao is a teenage inventor from the United States. When she heard about a problem with one city's water supply—the water contained the harmful substance lead—her reaction was to [4]_____ a [5]_____ that anyone could use to check the amount of lead in the water in their house. One thing the word *inventor* can mean, then, is a person who sees a problem and works to solve it.

Like many scientists, Rao thought that she could [6]_____ to finding a good solution to the problem through [7]_____— [8]_____ something together with other scientists. In addition to the positive effects that Rao's [9]_____ have had on the people who use them, her work might [10]_____ other young inventors by encouraging them to care enough about a problem to work toward a solution. In fact, Rao is one inventor who wants to inspire others. She holds educational events for young people to introduce them to scientific ideas.

C Complete the sentences with the correct form of the words from exercise A.

1. If you _____ someone, you make them believe they can do something.

2. _____ is the process of working together to achieve something.

3. A(n) _____ is a person who creates something new.

4. If you _____ to a project, you play a role in its success.

5. The Internet was a(n) _____ that changed the way people communicate.

6. Many people have an idea for something they want to _____; for example, a new app.

7. Young people have opportunities to _____ at school, such as on a project or on a team.

8. Companies sometimes begin with one goal that then _____ something else. Samsung, for example, sold noodles before it sold electronics.

9. Right now the technology department is _____ my computer. I hope they can fix it!

10. A(n) _____ can be a phone or laptop, but it can also be any piece of equipment made to do a certain task.

D PERSONALIZE Work in a group. Discuss the questions.

1. What **inventors** can you name? What did those people invent?
2. Very often, more than one person **contributes** to a new technology or idea. What kinds of skills do you think are helpful for successful **collaboration**?
3. Who are some people who have **inspired** you? How did they inspire you?

Gitanjali Rao at the 2022
Muhammad Ali Humanitarian
Awards in Kentucky, USA

B Listening Tech for Good

Critical Thinking **A** **ACTIVATE** Work with a partner. Discuss the questions.

1. An app is a program designed to perform specific tasks on a computer, smartphone, or other device. What are some tasks that apps can perform?
2. Why do people create apps?
3. What do you think "Tech for Good" means?

B **MAIN IDEAS** Listen to the conversation and take notes. Then answer the questions. 🔊

1. What are the speakers discussing?
   a. Apps they want to try on their phones
   b. Famous female inventors in history
   c. People using technology to help others

2. What was Gitanjali Rao's main goal?
   a. To get scientists to collaborate with her
   b. To teach other young people about technology
   c. To use technology to solve social problems

3. Why did the university students in Jordan develop apps?
   a. To help organizations provide online training
   b. To help their local community
   c. To show young people it's easy to do

C **DETAILS** Listen again and write GR for *Gitanjali Rao* or SJ for *students from Jordan*. 🔊

1. _____ Developed a device to detect lead in drinking water

2. _____ Developed an app to find public transportation

3. _____ Thought of an app to identify unkind words in text or email

4. _____ Wanted to help young people find jobs

5. _____ Worked with UNESCO to develop inventions

6. _____ Worked with 3M and UNICEF to develop inventions

D **FOCUSED LISTENING** Listen to the excerpts and write the verb phrases you hear. Then discuss the different meanings of the verb phrases. 🔊

1. She _____ science and technology to solve problems and to help people.

2. The app is called Kindly. They're still _____ it, . . .

3. She has _____ companies . . . to develop her inventions.

4. . . . the really cool thing is that the students are _____ their phones!

LISTENING SKILL   Recognize Opinions

When speakers give their opinions, they use certain words and phrases. Listen for the ideas that come after these expressions:

For me, . . .	*I'd say (that) . . .*	*In my view, . . .*
I believe that . . .	*If you ask me . . .*	*It seems to me (that) . . .*

If you ask me, *the younger generation has better solutions to world problems.*
I'd say that *cyberbullying is one of the biggest problems with the Internet.*

E Listen to excerpts from the conversation and choose the statements that are opinions. 🔊

1. a. An app to prevent cyberbullying is helpful.
   b. Cyberbullying can happen on social media.
2. a. Rao likes to collaborate.
   b. She will inspire more inventors.
3. a. Working on the apps from their phones was a good thing.
   b. The students in Jordan wanted to help with local problems.

F **EVALUATE** Work in a group. Discuss the questions and practice giving your opinions. | Critical Thinking

1. Do you think Rao is a genius?
2. What kind of opportunities did Rao need to develop her ideas?
3. Do you think collaboration in the technology industry is important? In other industries?
4. Do you think we will ever have too many apps?

▼ The Information Communications and Technology (ICT) sector, which includes the Internet and cellphones, is growing quickly in Jordan.

B Speaking

Critical Thinking | **A** **ANALYZE** With a partner, discuss what has happened or changed with each kind of technology in the box.

| apps | cameras | computers | the Internet | phones | TV |

A: What's changed with TV?
B: People watch shows on their phones now.

SPEAKING SKILL Give Reasons

It's important to give reasons to support your opinions or explain a situation. You can use *because* or *since* to introduce a reason. Notice that the reason clause can come after or before the main clause.

reason
*Cancer is a problem for doctors **because** it's really many diseases—not just one.*

reason
***Since** computers can read a lot of information very quickly, they might be able to discover new things.*

Here are some other phrases that introduce reasons:

*The website is slow **due to** the number of people who are on it.*
***Another reason for** my concern is the lack of privacy online.*

Phone booths from
the New York
World's Fair in 1964

B Read each statement and write A for *Agree* or D for *Disagree*. Then share your answers with a group. Give reasons for your opinions.

1. _____ You shouldn't check your phone when you're eating dinner with friends or family.

2. _____ Governments should provide better access to the Internet.

3. _____ You shouldn't share your personal information online.

4. _____ Schools should offer more classes in programming and app development.

5. _____ App developers should help solve people's problems, not just make games.

C **EXPLAIN** Look at the information. With a partner, take turns explaining the reasons the apps were developed. | Critical Thinking

Technology	Problem(s) solved
Autocorrect program	Making spelling or grammar mistakes
Tethys lead-detection device	Drinking water with high levels of lead
Kindly antibullying app	Sending messages that could make others feel bad
Apps made by students from Jordan	Finding public transportation, finding jobs

> *Since spelling and grammar mistakes are so common, the autocorrect program was created to fix these typos in our online messages.*

CRITICAL THINKING Synthesize

When you synthesize, you combine, or put together, information from two or more sources. Synthesizing can also involve combining new information with your own ideas and knowledge about a topic. Synthesizing can help you understand something better, find a solution to a problem, or think of new ways of doing something.

D Listen to an excerpt from each listening. Then discuss with a partner the reasons why the developers of the Kindly app probably want people to send example messages to them. 🔊 | Critical Thinking

E **SYNTHESIZE** Read the information and then discuss the question. | Critical Thinking

When you code, you write steps, or commands, for a computer to follow. People who code learn a special computer language such as Python or Java to "tell" the computer how to do something. Computers only do what programmers want if the programmers give logical commands, and writing logical commands takes a lot of practice.

What two things did the university students from Jordan learn how to do to create their successful apps?

Review

A **PRONUNCIATION** Say the words. Circle the ones that have long vowel sounds in the stressed syllable.

1. capable of (adj phr)
2. pattern (n)
3. privacy (n)
4. collaboration (n)
5. device (n)
6. lead (v)

B **VOCABULARY** Complete the sentences with the correct form of the words from exercise A.

1. In coding, _____ of 0s and 1s can be used.

2. Anyone is _____ coding with the right training.

3. Good communication is important for _____.

4. A class president _____ the class.

5. Companies that collect our data need to protect our _____.

6. Phones are so important even though they are small _____.

C **GRAMMAR** Think about how to complete the sentences with the present perfect. Then say the sentences aloud.

1. I have always . . .
2. In this class, we have already . . .
3. I have never . . .
4. So far this year, my family has . . .

D **SPEAKING SKILL** Give reasons for the statements.

1. You should never share your passwords.
2. Young people are good inventors.

RE-ASSESS What skills or language still need improvement?

Final Tasks

OPTION 1 Discuss human and machine intelligence

A In the listening on artificial intelligence, Dr. Ali says, "We have not achieved strong AI yet, and some people think we never will because they don't think AI will ever be able to think the same way humans can." Take notes on your answers to the following questions on a separate piece of paper.

1. What makes a human intelligent?
2. What makes a machine intelligent?
3. Do you think machines will ever be able to think the same way humans can?

COLLABORATION SKILL Acknowledge Ideas and Disagree Politely

It is good to show that you appreciate the ideas of others in your group. Here are some useful phrases.

That makes sense.　　　*I see what you mean.*
That's true.　　　　　　*That's a good/interesting idea.*

After you acknowledge their ideas, you might sometimes disagree with group members. You can use these phrases.

... but I'm not sure I agree.　　　*There might be another way to look at it, however.*
... but my viewpoint is ...　　　　*The way I see it is ...*

🛜 **ONLINE** During an online discussion, you can use emoji such as the thumbs-up or 100 to show you agree with ideas. However, if you disagree with someone in an online forum, it's better to tell them directly rather than use emoji.

B Discuss your ideas from exercise A with a small group. Be sure to acknowledge others' ideas, and if you disagree, do so politely. Share your group's most common and most unique ideas with the class.

ChatGPT is an AI chatbot that can have humanlike conversations and perform language-based tasks, such as writing emails and essays.

OPTION 2 Present a useful app

A MODEL Listen to a student talking about an app and answer the questions. 🔊

1. What is the name of the app?
    a. Chemistry Class
    b. Elements
    c. The Chemical Touch

2. Why does the student use it? Choose TWO reasons.
    a. She's in a chemistry class.
    b. She needs to memorize the periodic table.
    c. It's an easy way to view the periodic table.
    d. She needs to discover new elements for homework.

B ANALYZE THE MODEL Listen again and write what you hear. 🔊

1. Today _____ about an app called . . .

2. _____ brings up . . .

3. This app _____ to me in . . .

4. For these reasons, _____ this app . . .

C PLAN Think of an app that you can recommend to your classmates. Use the questions in exercise A and the phrases from exercise B to help you plan your presentation.

D PRACTICE AND PRESENT Practice presenting your app to a partner before you present it to a group of classmates.

A restaurant owner who is deaf uses an iPad app that allows her to make phone calls and to confirm reservations for her restaurant through a translation service with the hearing, in San Francisco, USA.

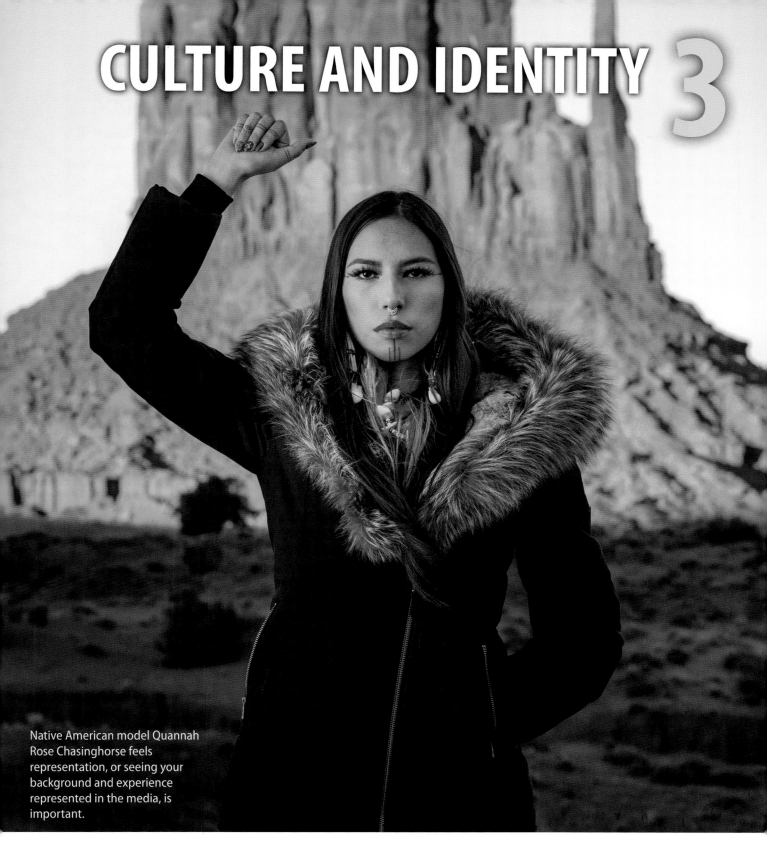

CULTURE AND IDENTITY 3

Native American model Quannah Rose Chasinghorse feels representation, or seeing your background and experience represented in the media, is important.

IN THIS UNIT, YOU WILL:

- Watch or listen to a lecture on a Mexican tradition
- Watch a video on the People of the Horse
- Listen to a conversation about travel and identity
- Discuss something popular from another culture OR Present your identity

THINK AND DISCUSS:

1. How often do you see people like you in TV shows, movies, or advertisements?

2. Why is it helpful to see people whose backgrounds are different from yours in the media?

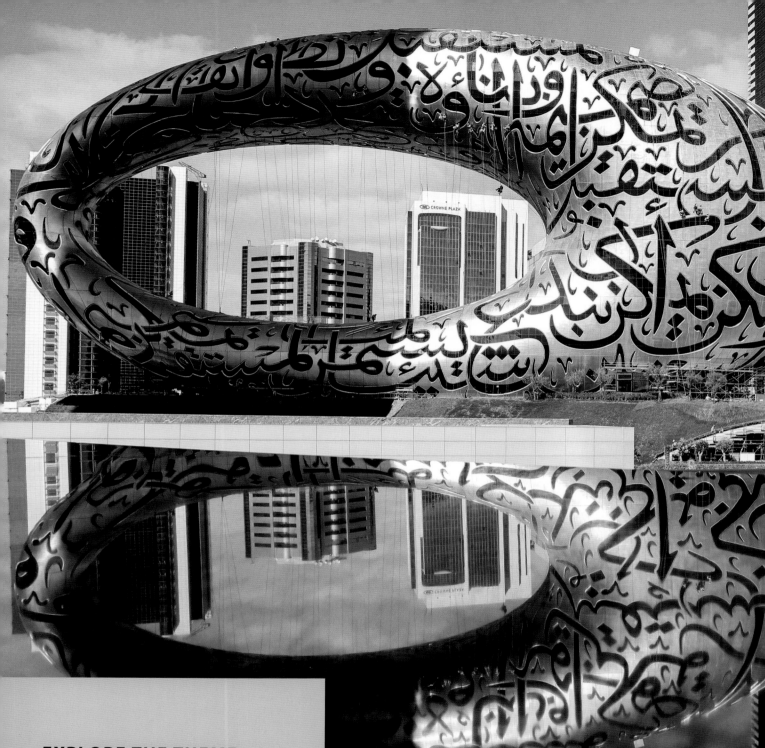

EXPLORE THE THEME

Read the information. Then discuss the questions.

1. Why do you think Arabic calligraphy was included as part of the design of the Museum of the Future?

2. What are some important museums or monuments in your country?

3. What other countries does your country share heritage with?

Cultural Heritage

Cultural heritage includes things we can see and touch, such as statues, monuments, and musical instruments.

The Museum of the Future in Dubai, United Arab Emirates

It also includes things we cannot see and touch. This intangible cultural heritage includes traditions, oral histories, performing arts, and knowledge passed down from earlier generations.

UNESCO (United Nations Educational, Scientific and Cultural Organization) has recognized almost seven hundred forms of intangible culture in one hundred forty countries—connected to one country or to multiple countries. Arabic calligraphy, for example, which forms the windows of the Museum of the Future in Dubai, United Arab Emirates, has been recognized as intangible cultural heritage of sixteen countries, including the UAE.

A Vocabulary

A Listen and repeat. Check the words you know. 🔊

ancestor (n)	**background** (n)	**connect** (v)	**involve** (v)	**tradition** (n)
aspect (n)	**bravery** (n)	**generation** (n)	**show off** (v phr)	**value** (n)

B **MEANING FROM CONTEXT** Listen and write the words you hear. Then think about each word's meaning. 🔊

COWBOY HERITAGE

The cowboy [1]_____ in Mexico began in the 1500s, when Spanish people brought the first cattle[1] there. The workers who took care of these animals were called *vaqueros*, from the Spanish word *vaca*, which means "cow." They wore big hats to keep the sun off their faces and high boots to protect their legs. Later, some Mexican vaqueros moved north into Texas, and their clothing became an [2]_____ of the cowboy culture in the United States, too. In fact, wearing cowboy hats and boots is a custom that younger [3]_____ of cowboys still continue in many parts of North America. Certain cowboy [4]_____ such as independence and respect are also important parts of the culture there.

These days, there are two kinds of cowboys in Mexico. Vaqueros work with cattle on the ranches, especially in the northern and western parts of the country. Their work [5]_____ riding horses just as their [6]_____ did, and they live outdoors for many months at a time. In addition, Mexico also has *charros*, and they're an important part of popular culture in Mexico. Charros wear beautiful cowboy clothing, ride horses, and [7]_____ their skills and [8]_____ in sporting events called *charreadas*. Most charros don't work on ranches, but their [9]_____ [10]_____ them to the cowboy heritage in Mexico.

[1]**cattle** (n) large animals raised for meat and milk, such as cows

◀ A Mexican cowboy showing off his skills during a charrería

C Choose the best word to complete each sentence.

1. An example of a family **background / tradition** is making a certain dish on a holiday.
2. Communication is an important **ancestor / aspect** of a teacher's job.
3. **Ancestors / Generations** are people from your family who lived a long time ago.
4. If you **connect / show off** a skill, you want people to see that you have the skill.
5. Celebrating holidays together helps family members **connect / involve** with each other.
6. A person's **background / bravery** influences who they are.
7. A person who shows **bravery / values** is willing to do something that scares them.
8. The **generation / tradition** you belong to includes the people around your same age.
9. Understanding a culture can **involve / show off** learning its music, language, art, or food.
10. I learned important **aspects / values** from my grandparents.

VOCABULARY SKILL   Noun and Adjective Suffixes

A suffix is a word ending that shows the form of a word.

                 noun   adjective

*People from my parents' genera**tion** sometimes have differ**ent** values than I do.*

Common noun suffixes include *-tion, -ence/-ance, -ity.*

      genera**tion**   differ**ence**   capabil**ity**

Common adjective suffixes include *-al, -ent/-ant, -able.*

      internation**al**   differ**ent**   cap**able**

D Complete the sentences with the correct nouns or adjectives from the box.

available	independence	nation	tradition
availability	independent	nationality	traditional

1. As they grow, children learn to be _____ from their parents.
2. Coffee is a _____ drink for breakfast in many places.
3. Giving money to children when they lose teeth is not a _____ in my culture.
4. If you are a citizen of Mexico, your _____ is Mexican.
5. Mexico gained _____ from Spain in 1821.
6. The cowboy hat is _____ in different sizes.
7. The _____ of some products at the grocery store hasn't been very good lately.
8. Canada is the second biggest _____ in the world in terms of size.

A Listening A Mexican Tradition

Critical Thinking **A** **ACTIVATE** You are going to hear a lecture about the national sport of Mexico. Work with a partner. Discuss these questions.

1. How are sports and culture connected? For example, are there certain sports that are popular in some countries or cultures? Or certain foods people eat while watching sports?
2. What are some values that sports teach?

B **MAIN IDEAS** Watch or listen to the lecture and write T for *True* or F for *False*. 🔊 ▶

1. _____ *Charrería* is a sport that involves people showing off their riding skills.
2. _____ Women riders are not officially a part of *charrería*.
3. _____ The riding skills in *charrería* come from a ranching culture and war.
4. _____ *Charrería* in the U.S. shows how sports connect people to their culture.
5. _____ Younger generations of riders learn important values from *charrería*.

NOTE-TAKING SKILL Use Abbreviations and Symbols

When you take notes, you don't have time to write out complete sentences. You can use abbreviations—short forms of words—and symbols.

There are many ways to abbreviate. It's important to develop a system that works for you. One way is to write only the first one or two syllables or only the consonants of the words.

Spanish—Span   Mexico—Mex   people—ppl   culture—cultr   national—nat'l

Here are some common symbols:

+ (and, also)   ↓ (decrease)   ↑ (increase)   ≠ (isn't/aren't)   w/ (with)

b/c (because)   e.g. (for example)   = (is/are, means)   ♂ (male/men)   ♀ (female/women)

C Match the abbreviations and symbols to words from the lecture.

1. _____ sprt   a. *charrería*
2. _____ charr   b. competition
3. _____ hist   c. connect
4. _____ ♂   d. cultural
5. _____ ♀   e. history
6. _____ cnnct   f. increased
7. _____ comp   g. men
8. _____ Mex Am   h. Mexican American
9. _____ cltrl   i. sport
10. _____ ↑   j. women

Members of the Flor de Gardenia horse-riding team perform in Snelling, California, USA.

D **DETAILS** Listen to the statements and take notes using abbreviations and symbols. Listen again and revise your notes so they are as short and clear as possible. 🔊

1. _____

_____

2. _____

_____

3. _____

_____

4. _____

_____

E **PERSONALIZE** Discuss the questions with a small group.

1. What is a popular sport in your country?
2. What food do people eat when they watch it?
3. Is music a part of the sport? If so, how?
4. What values does the sport support or teach?

A Speaking

Critical Thinking

A **EVALUATE** Hard work and respect are values that *charrería* teaches. Which of the following statements do you think are also true?

1. People who perform in *charreadas* need coordination, which is the ability to use different parts of the body together.
2. Precision, or being accurate, is important for female riders when they perform together.
3. *Charrería* is for extroverts—people who like to be around other people.

See Relative Pronouns as Subjects and Objects in the Appendix.

GRAMMAR FOR SPEAKING Adjective Clauses

Adjective clauses describe a noun—just as adjectives do. Notice how we can combine two simple sentences to form a complex sentence by using an adjective clause.

> *Rosa has a horse. The horse is nine years old.*
> *Rosa has a horse **that is nine years old**.*

A relative pronoun replaces the noun in an adjective clause. If it replaces a subject, use *who* or *that* for people and *that* or *which* for animals or things.

> subject   verb
> *People need coordination. <u>They</u> perform in* charreadas.

> subject
> pronoun verb
> *People **who perform in** charreadas need coordination.*

If the relative pronoun replaces an object, use *that* or *who* (or *whom* in formal speech) for people and *that* or *which* for animals or things.

> verb object
> *The hats are big.* Charros *wear <u>them</u>.*

> object
> pronoun   verb
> *The hats **that** charros **wear** are big.*

NOTE: In object adjective clauses, the relative pronoun is often omitted or left out.

> *One skill **(that) cowboys learn** is independence.*

B Unscramble the phrases to create sentences. There is ONE phrase you don't need in each.

1. the men / fought on horseback / who worked on ranches / worked on ranches

    _____

2. I wrote / for Mr. Azarian's class / this is the story / which I wrote it

    _____

3. old-fashioned / the riders / wear dresses / which are old-fashioned

    _____

4. that I watched / the soccer match / on Saturday it was exciting / on Saturday was exciting

    _____

C Combine the sentences using an adjective clause.

1. The professor gave a lecture about intangible cultural heritage. The lecture was very popular.

   _____

2. Hard work is a value. I learned it from my parents.

   _____

3. My ancestors were immigrants. They came from Ireland.

   _____

4. Drinking tea is a tradition. Many cultures share it.

   _____

5. Animals can represent values such as strength and wisdom. People want these values.

   _____

D **PERSONALIZE** Work with a partner. Finish each sentence so that it is true for you.

1. I have family members who . . .
2. I enjoy watching shows that . . .
3. A job that I can imagine doing is . . .
4. One thing I should read more about is . . .
5. I admire people who . . .

SPEAKING SKILL Define Unfamiliar Terms

When you use words or phrases that others might not know, it's a good idea to define them. You can define terms with *be* and *This/It means*.

> It's called <u>charrería</u>, and **it's the national sport** of Mexico.
> The women ride <u>sidesaddle</u>. **This means both legs are on one side of the horse**.

Another way to define a term is with a noun and an adjective clause.

> <u>UNESCO</u> is **an organization that works to build peace in the world**.

E Underline the word that might be unfamiliar in each sentence. Then work with a partner. Write a definition for each word. Use a dictionary if necessary.

1. One rider had an especially beautiful saddle on her horse.
2. Self-reliance is an important skill to learn before you leave home.
3. Every year there is a championship for the best teams.
4. The riders can feel the adrenaline in their bodies.
5. Values are an intangible aspect of a culture.

F **DISCOVER** Work with a partner. Student A will read about *paniolos*. Student B will read about *gauchos*. As you read, take brief notes to answer the questions below. Look up any unfamiliar words so you can explain them.

1. What kind of cowboy is the paragraph about? Where do these cowboys live?
2. What kind of work does/did this kind of cowboy do?
3. How is life for these cowboys different now than in the past?

Student A
Paniolos

Hawaii has traditional cowboys called *paniolos*. The first cattle in Hawaii were a gift to the king in 1793. Many years later, the first three cowboys came to Hawaii. They were Mexican men who were living in California at the time. The king invited them to the island to control the growing population of cattle and also to teach cattle-handling skills to the local people. Because those first cowboys spoke Spanish (*español*), Hawaiians gave them the name *paniolo*. Now there are only a few large ranches in Hawaii, and the last *paniolos* are very old, but people still enjoy learning about Hawaiian cowboy culture.

Student B
Gauchos

Gauchos are the cowboys of Brazil, Argentina, and Uruguay. *Gauchos* were working in those countries as early as the 1700s. Today, people still admire *gauchos* for their independence, bravery, and skills—especially their horseback riding. *Gauchos* are the subject of many stories and legends, but in real life, most *gauchos* were very poor. Usually, the only things they owned were their clothing and their horses. Today *gauchos* still take care of cattle in South America, but their lives are more prosperous than they were in the past. Now most of them receive a steady salary, and they no longer have to move from place to place to find work.

Women in Argentina continue the *gaucho* tradition.

G **EXPLAIN** Now close your books and take turns telling each other about the kind of cowboy you read about. Use your notes to help you. Define any unfamiliar terms for your partner.

The People of the Horse

▲ Navajo horse trainer
Clayson Benally

A Horses are important to Native Americans. They represent tradition and help to pass down values, such as caring for other living beings on Earth. Watch the video and check the points the speaker makes. ▶

Horses . . .

a. ☐ tell you about the weather.
b. ☐ understand a person's character.
c. ☐ don't complain about carrying you.
d. ☐ teach people things.
e. ☐ don't care about your problems.
f. ☐ are good friends.

B Watch again. Choose the best meaning for the underlined word. Use a dictionary if necessary. ▶

1. They don't <u>judge</u> you.

   a. have an opinion about   b. do something wrong to

2. They protect little kids because they're so <u>innocent</u>.

   a. young, easily harmed   b. inexperienced, without knowledge of bad things

3. At the same time, they're just as <u>naughty</u>.

   a. acting somewhat badly   b. hurting someone badly

C **PERSONALIZE** Work in a small group. Discuss the questions.

1. Did anything in the video surprise you?
2. Which animals are important to people in your culture? Why?
3. In your opinion, do animals have feelings or emotions like humans? Explain.

Vocabulary

A **MEANING FROM CONTEXT** Listen and notice the words in blue. Think about the meaning of each word and write it next to its definition on the next page. Then check if each statement is true for you. Compare your answers with a partner. 🔊

Culture Survey	Yes	No
1. I can think of a **custom** or **belief** in my culture that might be unique in the world.		
2. I know of at least one **accomplishment** of a scientist, artist, athlete, or other well-known person from my country.		
3. My background is a large part of my current **identity**, or how I see myself.		
4. I can think of at least one **similarity** between my culture and another culture and at least one important difference.		
5. I think people in my country **tend to** welcome visitors from other countries and **treat** them well.		
6. I can think of an aspect of the way parents **raise** children in my culture that might surprise people from other cultures.		
7. I had a **chance** to hear stories from my family as I grew up that kept important memories alive or told lessons.		
8. I feel like I come from one place and am **local** to another place.		

At Kurentovanje, Slovenia's festival to welcome spring, people dress in sheeplike costumes with bells. It is believed to be good luck for one of these *Kurenti* to visit your house, and the custom is recognized by UNESCO as intangible cultural heritage.

1. _____ (n) an aspect or characteristic that is nearly the same

2. _____ (n) an idea that is considered to be true

3. _____ (n) an achievement; something that has been done successfully

4. _____ (n) our sense of ourselves and who we are

5. _____ (n) a way of acting or doing something that is common in a culture

6. _____ (v) to care for and educate one's children

7. _____ (adj) existing in or belonging to a certain area or neighborhood

8. _____ (v phr) to be likely to do a particular thing

9. _____ (n) the possibility to do something; the opportunity

10. _____ (v) to behave toward someone in a particular way

B Complete the conversations with the correct form of the words from exercise A.

1. A: Did you grow up with any specific _____?

   B: Yes, my parents _____ me to believe in the value of hard work.

2. A: Is having a big wedding a _____ in your country?

   B: No, it's more of a _____ tradition. There are smaller weddings in some parts of the country.

3. A: The teachers in my school _____ assign a lot of reading.

   B: That's a _____ between our schools. My teachers do the same thing.

4. A: My _____ is complicated because I have had the _____ to live in two different cultures.

   B: So you see both cultures as parts of who you are!

5. A: Will you _____ me differently if I win a Nobel Prize someday?

   B: No, I will act the same toward you, but I will be very proud of your _____!

C **RATE** Read the statements about traveling. Note how much you agree with each one and then discuss with a partner. | Critical Thinking

strongly disagree   neutral   strongly agree

1   2   3   4   5

1. _____ People around the world have more **similarities** than differences.

2. _____ Thanks to the Internet, I don't need to travel to have a **chance** to meet people around the world.

3. _____ Traveling and having new experiences can change people's **beliefs** about the world.

4. _____ I enjoy eating **local** foods when I travel, especially if it's something unusual for me.

5. _____ Everywhere that I have traveled, people have **treated** me well.

Listening Travel and Identity

Critical Thinking | **A** **ACTIVATE** Discuss the questions with a partner.

1. What are some important parts of your identity?
2. Do different people see you in different ways? Explain.
3. How does your identity affect your travel experiences in other countries?

LISTENING SKILL Ask Questions

Being an active listener is important at school, work, and in everyday life. One way to be an active listener is to ask yourself questions while you are listening.

- Ask questions to prepare for the kind of information that will probably come next.
- Ask how the information you hear compares with other information you have heard or read. This can help you evaluate the new information.
- Think about the source. Is the speaker an expert in the field? Is the information recent? What is the speaker's purpose?

For example, you hear: *"What if I told you that there is a woman who has traveled to every country on Earth . . . And she was only thirty-five when she made it to the last country on her list?"*

You could ask yourself: *Who is she?* Or think: *Why did she do that?* You might also ask yourself why the speaker is telling you this.

B **MAIN IDEAS** Listen to a conversation about a world traveler and answer the questions. 🔊

1. Which culture or cultures are important to Jessica Nabongo's identity?
   a. American
   b. Ugandan
   c. both American and Ugandan

2. Why is Nabongo's accomplishment special, according to the man? Choose TWO answers.
   a. Not many people have done it.
   b. She did everything in one year.
   c. Next, she can go to outer space.
   d. She's the first Black woman to do it.

3. Why did Nabongo want to visit every country?
   a. To become world famous
   b. To learn about each one
   c. To try every kind of food

C **DETAILS** Listen again. Write T for *True* or F for *False*. Then correct the false sentences. 🔊

1. _____ Jessica Nabongo was 25 years old when she visited the last country on her list.

2. _____ Some Ugandans treat Nabongo differently from native African people.

3. _____ After Nabongo graduated in 2005, she moved to Japan.

4. _____ Nabongo started writing a travel blog to stay connected with her friends and family.

5. _____ Nabongo enjoys the food in the country of Georgia.

D **FOCUSED LISTENING** Listen and write the words you hear. What kind of words are these? Can any be omitted? 🔊

1. What if I told you that there is a woman _____ has traveled to every country on Earth?

2. There are more people _____ have traveled to outer space than to every country on Earth!

3. She wanted to do the same thing _____ he had done.

Jessica Nabongo describes herself as "Afropolitan."

B | Speaking

Critical Thinking **A** **COMPARE** Work with a partner. How are these customs similar to or different from customs in your country or culture? Explain.

- In Germany and Japan, it is important to be punctual, or on time.
- People take off their shoes before they enter someone's home in China and Korea.
- In India, you should eat everything on your plate to show that you enjoyed the food.

CRITICAL THINKING Consider Different Perspectives

People bring their own perspective to a topic. Notice how these speakers differ in how they see the same situation.

Speaker A: *Our dinner guests were rather impolite. They left some food on their plates.*
Speaker B: *Our dinner guests were very polite. They left a little food on their plates.*

For Speaker A, leaving some food on a plate could mean the dinner guests did not like the food. For Speaker B, it could mean the guests had plenty to eat.

Critical Thinking **B** Work with a partner. For each conversation, discuss the possible perspective of Speaker A. Then match each conversation to a type of custom.

1. _____ A: I can't believe the teacher called on me in class! I didn't even raise my hand.
   B: I am used to that. Teachers here do it all the time.

2. _____ A: I feel terrible. Everyone else at the wedding gave money to the bride.
   B: But you gave the couple a nice gift. Don't feel bad.

3. _____ A: The waiter doesn't look happy. Were we supposed to leave him a tip?
   B: No, most people don't tip here. He was probably unhappy about something else.

4. _____ A: She isn't late for class. Class only started 15 minutes ago.
   B: Fifteen minutes is pretty late! I usually arrive a few minutes early.

5. _____ A: That was odd. Charlie sat in the front seat with the taxi driver!
   B: True, but there were three of us. He probably felt more comfortable in the front.

a. classroom culture   c. giving gifts   e. being on time

b. personal space   d. leaving a tip

PRONUNCIATION The Vowel Sound /ɜr/

🔊 The vowel sound /ɜr/ is the same as the *-ir* in *bird*. The sound is spelled in several ways.

   *h**er***   *w**or**d*   *h**ur**t*   *l**ear**n*   *sh**ir**t*

Notice how the vowel sound in each pair of words is different.

   *We should **turn** left at the corner.*   *This piece of paper is **torn**.*
   *You need to **stir** the soup.*   *That **star** is bright.*
   *I **work** in that office building.*   *Let's **walk** another block.*

A local guide educates tourists in the At-Turaif visitor's center in Saudi Arabia. Traveling is a great way to learn about other cultures.

C Listen and choose the word you hear. Then work with a partner. Take turns saying one word of each pair and having your partner point to the words they hear. 🔊

1. a. burn   b. born
2. a. shirts   b. shorts
3. a. hurt   b. heart
4. a. bird   b. bored
5. a. heard   b. hard
6. a. were   b. war

D Work with a partner. Ask each question with one of the words in parentheses. Your partner will choose the best answer.

1. Are you buying new (shirts / shorts)?
   a. Yes, I need some with long sleeves.
   b. Yes, it's too hot for long pants.

2. Did you have to (work / walk) today?
   a. No, today was my day off.
   b. No, my friend gave me a ride.

3. How much did you (learn / loan) today?
   a. A lot! I need to review my notes.
   b. Not much. People don't seem to need money right now.

4. Did you say you (were / wore) a flower?
   a. Yes, in a school play when I was five years old.
   b. Yes, I wore one in my hair.

5. Do you plant flowers (yearly / early)?
   a. No, not every year.
   b. Yes, at the beginning of spring.

Review

A VOCABULARY

1. Write a sentence with each word: *connection, ancestor, tend to*.
2. Choose the word with the same meaning as the word in **bold**.

   a. **tradition**   background / belief / custom

   b. **value**   belief / identity / accomplishment

   c. **aspect**   part / history / feeling

B PRONUNCIATION Underline the /ɜr/ vowel sounds in each sentence. Then say the sentences.

1. Is that a bird that I heard?
2. Getting a sunburn really hurts.
3. He's learning to make shirts.
4. I didn't turn in my work on time.

C GRAMMAR Say sentences with adjective clauses.

1. This is the class . . .
2. My best friend is the person . . .
3. My shoes are the ones . . .
4. I enjoy eating foods . . .

D SPEAKING SKILL Underline the explanations of words.

1. Respect for older people is a core, or central, belief in my culture.
2. My mother makes the best *pad see ew*, which is a Thai noodle dish.
3. The people at the airport scrutinized my passport, which means they looked at it carefully.

RE-ASSESS What skills or language still need improvement?

Final Tasks

OPTION 1 Discuss something popular from another culture

A **BRAINSTORM** Think of something that is from another culture but is popular in your country or culture. Use an idea from the categories below or your own idea. List some possible reasons for its popularity.

books	food	music	television
fashion	movies	sports	video games

B Look at your list of reasons from exercise A. Underline words that might not be familiar to everyone. Think of ways to define those unfamiliar words.

> *K-pop music might be popular in my country because many K-pop group members become <u>idols</u>. An idol is someone who other people admire very much.*

C Work in a small group. Share things from other cultures that are popular in your culture. Define any unfamiliar terms and practice active listening.

D After the discussion, consider these questions:

- How do you feel about how well you expressed your ideas?
- Did you use the skills and language from this unit?

Holi, or the festival of colors, is an Indian tradition for welcoming spring. It has spread to other countries around the world.

OPTION 2 Present your identity

A **MODEL** Listen to someone talking about different ways she is viewed and complete the chart with the views. ONE is extra. 🔊

How people in her hometown saw her	How she sees herself	How people in her new city see her

a. a good student

b. fashionable

c. funny

d. polite

e. poor

f. shy

B **ANALYZE THE MODEL** Listen again and answer the questions. 🔊

1. How do the people around the speaker form an opinion of her?
2. Does the speaker always see herself as others see her? Explain.
3. Does the speaker usually understand why people see her a certain way?

C **PLAN** Think about how different people see you and how you see yourself. Take notes.

D Read the Presentation Skill box. What key words and ideas will you repeat or emphasize in your presentation? Are there synonyms for key words that you can use?

PRESENTATION SKILL Repeat and Emphasize

When you give a presentation, it's helpful to repeat and emphasize the most important ideas.

*This brings us back to the idea of sharing our **perspectives**. If you understand where your **viewpoint** comes from, you can help your audience understand you better. For example, my **perspective** on what it means to be "on time" comes from my cultural background.*

Notice how the speaker repeats or emphasizes the key ideas of *perspective* and *viewpoint*.

E **PRACTICE AND PRESENT** Practice giving your presentation to a partner before you give it to the class.

Pomegranates have anticancer properties and can improve heart conditions like high blood pressure.

IN THIS UNIT, YOU WILL:

- Listen to a conversation about food psychology
- Watch a video on making small changes to your diet
- Watch or listen to a talk on culinary medicine
- Discuss how grocery stores affect consumers
  OR Debate whether cooking should be taught in schools

THINK AND DISCUSS:

1. Do you like pomegranates?
2. What other foods have major health benefits?
3. How could supermarkets make fruits and vegetables more appealing to customers?

Read the information. Then discuss the questions.

1. What is *hidden water*, or *virtual water*?

2. How many gallons of water are needed to produce a cup of tea? A pound of avocados?

3. Which kind of diet requires more water: a mostly vegetarian diet or a diet that includes meat? Why?

4. Does any of the information surprise you? Will it cause you to change any of your eating and drinking habits?

Hidden Water

The world uses trillions of gallons of virtual water. When you serve a pound[1] of beef, you are also serving 1,857 gallons[2] of water. A cup of coffee? That's 37 gallons, which is enough water to fill the average bathtub. This is how much fresh water we use without realizing it. It's called virtual water, or hidden water: the amount of water we need to produce something.

---

[1]one pound = 454 grams
[2]one gallon = 3.785 liters

ANIMAL PRODUCTS
Virtual-water totals include the amount of water, in gallons, used to raise the animals and turn them into a food product (e.g., making milk into cheese or putting eggs in a box).

589
PROCESSED CHEESE

400
EGGS

371
FRESH CHEESE

138
YOGURT

MEAT
The virtual water for meat is the water the animals drink and the water used to grow their food and clean their living areas.

1,857
GALLONS OF WATER USED TO PRODUCE ONE POUND OF BEEF

469
CHICKEN

FRUITS AND VEGETABLES

Both rainwater and irrigation water are included in the virtual-water totals for fruits and vegetables.

NUTS AND SEEDS

Tree nuts need a lot of water. Seeds, however, require much less water than nuts, and the water used often produces fruits, vegetables, and seeds to eat.

1,092
PISTACHIOS

902
ALMONDS

527
WALNUTS

382
HAZELNUTS

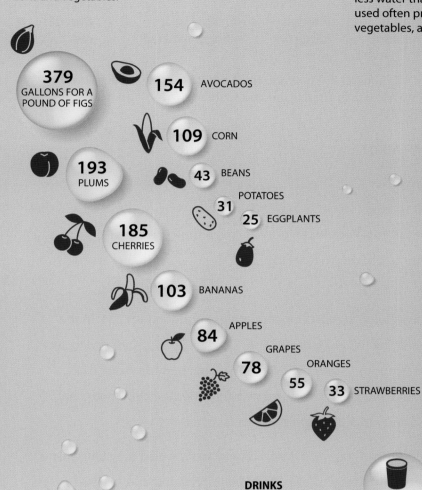

379
GALLONS FOR A POUND OF FIGS

154 AVOCADOS

109 CORN

43 BEANS

POTATOES
31

25 EGGPLANTS

193
PLUMS

185
CHERRIES

103 BANANAS

APPLES
84

GRAPES
78

ORANGES
55

33 STRAWBERRIES

46
SUNFLOWERS

101
ONE GLASS OF ALMOND MILK

14
WATERMELONS

12
PUMPKINS

DRINKS

53
ONE GLASS OF MILK

37
ONE CUP OF COFFEE

18
ONE GLASS OF SOY MILK

9
ONE CUP OF TEA

WHY MEAT USES MORE WATER

A human diet that regularly includes meat requires 60 percent more water than a mostly vegetarian diet. The graphic on the right shows the amount of water needed to raise an average cow, which takes about three years.

808,400
GALLONS FOR 18,700 POUNDS OF FEED

+

6,300
GALLONS FOR DRINKING

+

1,900
GALLONS FOR CLEANING

=

816,600
GALLONS USED DURING THE LIFE OF THE ANIMAL

Sources: Arjen Y. Hoekstra and Ashok K. Chapagain, *Globalization of Water*; Water Footprint Network, University of Twente, Netherlands, Waterfootprint.org

A Vocabulary

A Listen and repeat. Check the words you know. 🔊

apply (v)	**display** (v)	**interest** (v)	**label** (n)	**purchase** (v)
description (n)	**hunger** (n)	**judge** (v)	**powerful** (adj)	**react** (v)

B **MEANING FROM CONTEXT** Look at the text and think whether each missing word is probably a noun, a verb, or an adjective. Then listen and write the words you hear. 🔊

THE MILKSHAKE EXPERIMENT

Foods in stores often have ¹_____ on them that show things like how much fat, sugar, and salt the foods have. Some restaurants now ²_____ that information on their menus, too. People can use labels like these to ³_____ how healthy a food is and to decide whether to ⁴_____ it. Can labels do more than this, though?

An experiment by psychologist Alia Crum and others suggests they can. In the experiment, participants drank two milkshakes. The ⁵_____ of one included the words "creamy" and "smooth . . . and delicious." The label said the shake had 620 calories and 30 grams of fat. The other shake was described as "light [and] healthy." According to the label, it had just 140 calories and no fat at all.

After participants drank the "creamy" shake, a blood test showed they felt satisfied and full. In contrast, after the "healthy" shake, blood tests indicated that people felt less full. This should not seem surprising; after all, foods with more calories *should* reduce people's ⁶_____ more. However, the two milkshakes were the same except for their labels. In other words, the only reason people felt fuller or less full was because the *labels* were different.

This result shows that Crum's experiment is important. Businesses can use food labels and descriptions in several ⁷_____ ways. They can use them to change how people think about foods. They can use them to ⁸_____ people in foods. Companies might even be able to ⁹_____ what they have learned from Crum's experiment and use labels to affect how people's bodies ¹⁰_____ to foods.

C Write each word from exercise A next to its definition.

1. _____ (n) a piece of paper on a product that gives information about it

2. _____ (n) an explanation of what a person or thing is like

3. _____ (adj) having control and the ability to affect people or situations

4. _____ (n) the feeling of needing to eat because you are not full

5. _____ (v) to buy

6. _____ (v) to make a person want to learn more

7. _____ (v) to put something in a place that is easy for people to see

8. _____ (v) to say, do, or feel something because of something that happened

9. _____ (v) to think about a person or thing and form an opinion

10. _____ (v) to use a tool or something that you have learned in a new situation

VOCABULARY SKILL   Parts of Speech

Some words can be both nouns and verbs. You can look at how the word is used in the sentence to recognize the part of speech.

Remember that subjects and objects are nouns or pronouns. Verbs come after the subject and before the object.

noun
*A tiny **label** can be hard to read.*

verb
*We should **label** these products.*

D Read the sentences. Write N if the underlined word is a *Noun* or V if it's a *Verb*.

1. _____ Should we <u>purchase</u> these, or should we pick something else?

2. _____ What can I bring you to <u>drink</u> while you decide what to order?

3. _____ I <u>love</u> Spanish and Italian food, so it's my dream to go to Spain and Italy.

4. _____ Our waiter was friendly, but he couldn't <u>answer</u> any of our questions.

5. _____ The report said there was an <u>increase</u> in how hungry participants were.

6. _____ To save money, <u>plan</u> what you'll cook each week.

E Complete these tasks with a partner. Use a dictionary if necessary.

1. Compare and discuss your answers to exercise D.
2. Mark one other word in each sentence of exercise D that could also be a noun or verb.
3. Choose THREE words from task 2 and make sentences using them. Ask another pair of students whether your chosen words are nouns or verbs in your sentences.

Listening Food Psychology

Critical Thinking | **A** **ACTIVATE** Read the statements. Then discuss the questions in a group.

> *I usually order the cheapest item because I think it will be the best value.*
> *I want to enjoy eating out, so I order something that I can't easily make at home.*
> *I don't think much about what to order. I often just get the same as my friends.*
> *I get something small for my entrée. I want to make sure I save room for dessert!*

1. Which statements sound most and least like you when you go to a restaurant? Why?
2. How often do you eat at a restaurant? Would you like to eat out more? Why or why not?

B **MAIN IDEAS** Listen to a conversation and take notes. Then complete the summary using FIVE phrases from the box. The other phrases are extra. 🔊

important decisions	popular restaurants	reasonable price	three friends
pizza place	positive descriptions	specific colors	various ways

Some students are having lunch together at a ¹_____ after attending a lecture. The ²_____ discuss what they learned about ³_____ that restaurants can affect how customers act and what they order. These methods include using ⁴_____, displaying photos, and giving detailed and ⁵_____ of the dishes on the menu. At the end of their discussion, they share what they feel about the information they learned as well as what they can do with it.

▼ People who own and manage restaurants in Japan say that displaying plastic copies of food in a window brings in more customers.

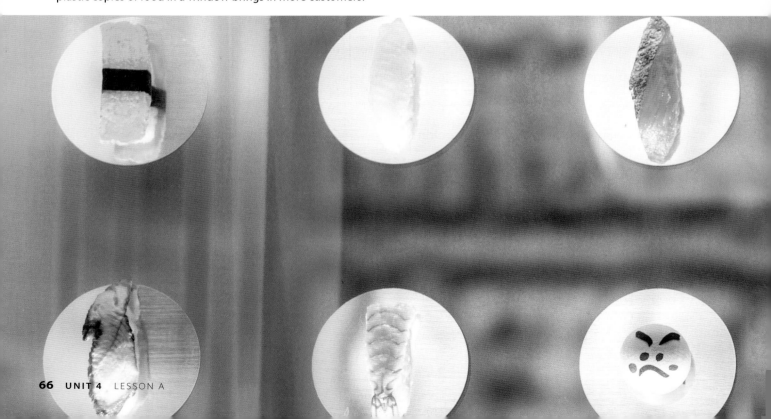

C **DETAILS** Listen again. Number the ideas in the order the speakers discuss them (1–7). 🔊

a. _____ Customers spend less money at restaurants that include dollar signs on their menus.

b. _____ Delicious-sounding descriptions are one way restaurants interest people in their food.

c. _____ Photographs of food on menus can increase sales at restaurants by up to one-third.

d. _____ If people know how restaurants try to affect them, they can think before they react.

e. _____ People feel prices ending with 95 or 99 are "friendly" and these dishes are good value.

f. _____ Restaurants may highlight certain dishes on their menus that are "high-margin."

g. _____ The color red can make people feel hungry; yellow can make them want to leave.

D **FOCUSED LISTENING** Listen and complete each expression with ONE word. 🔊

1. That's a pretty clever way to use photos and labels **in my** _____!

2. **How do you** _____ **about** the way restaurants use psychology to try to affect people?

3. I don't like it, **to be** _____. It feels wrong.

4. **Do you have a different** _____, Lydia?

5. On the other hand, **I'd** _____ **that** this kind of knowledge is pretty powerful.

E **PERSONALIZE** Work in a group. Discuss the questions.

1. Think about the last time you ate out. In what ways did the restaurant or café try to affect your choice about what to order?

2. How do you feel about companies using psychology to affect your choices about what to buy?

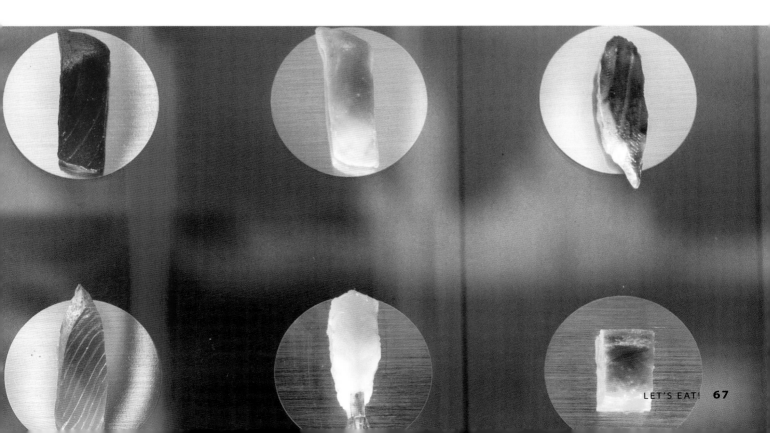

A Speaking

Critical Thinking

A EVALUATE In the listening, you heard the students talk about aspects of menu design. Discuss the questions with a small group.

1. How is viewing a menu on your phone different from viewing a menu you can hold and open?
2. Do you prefer to read a digital menu or a paper one?
3. With QR code menus, some restaurants allow their guests to order and pay online. What are the advantages and disadvantages of this?

See Forms of the Passive Voice in the Appendix.

GRAMMAR FOR SPEAKING   Active vs. Passive Voice

In the active voice, the subject of a sentence performs, or does, the action.

    subject   verb
*Companies sometimes **give** free samples to customers.*

In the passive voice, the subject receives the action.

        subject   verb
*Sometimes, customers **are given** free samples to interest them.*

We form the passive voice with the verb *be* plus the past participle of the main verb. Only the verb *be* changes to show when the action happens.

    *Our bodies **are affected** by our minds.*
    *These grapes **were grown** in Chile.*
    *How **should** these vegetables **be cooked**?*

We often use the passive voice to talk about processes or an action when the person doing the action is not important.

    *Next, labels **are attached** to each can of vegetables.*

We use *by* with the passive voice when we want to specify who or what does the action.

    *The blood samples **were taken** <u>by nurses</u>.*

B Underline each verb in the active voice. Circle each verb in the passive voice.

1. Most of my friends go grocery shopping at least once or twice a week.
2. I get fresh eggs from my neighbor every day. Her hens lay them.
3. People love burgers in my country. They can be eaten for lunch or dinner.
4. Some people say you should have breakfast every day, but I rarely do.
5. I ordered a curry for lunch. It was made with potatoes and cauliflower.

C Complete these sentences so they are true for you. Share your answers with a partner.

1. My favorite book was written by _____.
2. The best meal I've ever had was cooked by _____.
3. The last time I had my hair cut, it was cut by _____.
4. When I need a ride somewhere, I am usually driven by _____.

D Change these sentences from active voice to passive voice.

1. We need water to produce nearly everything.

   _____

2. Some restaurants allow their guests to order and pay online.

   _____

3. Restaurants can hire menu engineers to improve their menus.

   _____

4. They reopened the restaurant last month.

   _____

5. Farmers first plant the seeds.

   _____

E **APPLY** Work with a partner. Discuss which phrases from the box best complete each description. Then discuss what foods and/or drinks are described. | Critical Thinking

are buttered	are put	is cooked	is made	is spread
are often grown	can also be used	~~is drunk~~	is poured	may be added

1. In most places and by most people, this colorless liquid _____*is drunk*_____ more often than any other. It _____ in many other ways, including for cooking, cleaning, and washing.

2. Bread dough, which is a mix of flour, water, and yeast, _____ into a circle. Tomato sauce _____ on top of the dough along with cheese and other ingredients. Then the dough _____ in a very hot oven.

3. These beans _____ in countries like Brazil, Colombia, and Ethiopia. A machine roasts the beans until they turn brown and grinds them into very small pieces. Finally, very hot water _____ over the ground beans to make a popular drink.

4. Two slices of bread _____ and then cheese and meat _____ between the slices. Other things _____ too, such as mayonnaise, lettuce, or tomato.

F **BRAINSTORM** Work in a group. Discuss how to describe a well-known food or drink using the passive voice like the examples in exercise E. Share your description with the class. Can other students guess the food or drink? | Critical Thinking

SPEAKING SKILL   Give and Ask for Opinions

There are many expressions you can use to give your opinion:

In my opinion, . . .   *In my view, . . .*   *I'd say (that) . . .*
I think (that) . . .   *I feel (that) . . .*   *To be honest, . . .*

You can support your opinions with facts, examples, or personal experience:

*In my opinion, it's better to eat home-cooked meals because research shows that
restaurant meals can have too much salt and fat.*

Here are expressions for asking people for their opinions:

How do you feel about . . . ?   *In your opinion, . . . ?*
What do you think of/about . . . ?

🔊 **ONLINE** Some people may feel more comfortable giving their opinions in the chat
box. It's a good idea to let people know that they can do this. Don't forget to check chat
comments often. If you cannot see the comments, ask someone to read them to you.

G Underline the expressions in the conversation for giving or asking for opinions. Then practice
saying the conversation with a partner.

Manny: How do you feel about Indian food?

Alisa: I love it! It's probably my favorite kind of food.

Manny: Really? For some reason, I felt that you wouldn't like spicy food.

Alisa: Well, I don't like it to be *really* spicy, but I think a little bit of heat is great!
Besides, not all Indian food is spicy.

Manny: That's true. So, what is it about Indian food that you love so much?

Alisa: I'd say that it's the variety of healthy and delicious vegetarian dishes. I don't eat meat,
you see.

Critical Thinking **H** **EXPLAIN** Have conversations about the topics with a group. Practice asking for, giving, and
supporting your opinions.

- the most popular food in the world
- the worst thing for people to eat
- the cheapest good restaurant near the school
- the best thing to eat when you are really hungry

A: *What do you think is the most popular food in the world?*

B: *I feel it's probably pizza. As far as I know, everyone likes it.*

C: *You might be right, but what do you think about sushi? Isn't that just as popular?*

Sugary foods ▶
are one of the
worst things for
your teeth.

Video

Alex Sigrist: Small Changes

greenhouse gases (n phr) gases that trap heat
serving (n) an amount of food for one person
vegan (n) someone who does not eat any animal products

vegetarian (adj) related to not eating meat
compromise (n) a middle state between two different opinions or actions

▲ What you eat affects the planet.

A Watch the video. Check (✓) the TWO opinions you think Alex Sigrist would agree with. ▶

1. _____ Changing what you eat is an effective way to help the planet.

2. _____ Raising some animals is better for the planet than others.

3. _____ To reduce climate change, everybody must stop eating meat.

B Watch again. Complete each statement with a number from the box. ONE number is extra. ▶

| 1 | 2 | 5 | 15 | 25 | 60 | 330 | 2050 |

1. A United Nations (UN) report says about _____ percent of greenhouse gases, which are the cause of global warming, come from farming.

2. A serving of beef produces _____ grams of carbon emissions, which is the same as driving _____ minutes in a car. On the other hand, a serving of chicken produces just _____ grams.

3. If everyone followed the Mediterranean diet, there would be a _____ percent drop in greenhouse gases by _____, which is like taking _____ billion cars off the roads.

C **EXPLAIN** Mark an X on the line to show what you will do as a result of watching this video. Then join a small group. Take turns expressing and supporting your opinions.

Critical Thinking

I will completely change what I eat ◄————————————————► I will not change what I eat at all

B Vocabulary

A MEANING FROM CONTEXT Listen to the information. Think about the meaning of each word in blue, and then complete the definitions with the correct form of the words. 🔊

FOOD FOR HEALTH

If improving your **nutrition** and becoming healthier are among your goals, you might benefit from the help of a nutritionist. Our nutritionists have special training and can **advise** you on **recipes** and meal ideas that are not only healthy but cheap and easy to make, too.

Are you sick? Instead of just taking your medicine every day and waiting to get better, what if the food you eat could help in the **treatment** of your **illness**? Call us to learn a new **approach** that will teach you how to **combine** healthy cooking with the other things you do to stay in good health.

You know processed food is unhealthy, but do you know which foods are processed and which are not? Our new app solves this **issue** and is super **convenient** to use. Simply take a photo of a food and wait for the result. A green light means the food is unprocessed and natural; yellow means it is lightly processed but OK to eat; and red means it is processed heavily and should be avoided. The app won't make **suggestions** about what to eat, but it can help you make better decisions.

1. A(n) _____ (n) is a list of instructions that explain how to cook certain dishes.

2. A(n) _____ (n) is a health problem such as a cold, diabetes, or heart disease.

3. A(n) _____ (n) is a way of doing something or thinking about something.

4. A(n) _____ (n) is an idea, plan, or action that people should consider or do.

5. A(n) _____ (n) is any kind of problem that people have to deal with.

6. A(n) _____ (n) is anything a doctor does or recommends to help a patient.

7. _____ (n) is the food your body needs in order to grow or be healthy.

8. If you _____ (v) someone, you tell them what they could or should do.

9. Something that is _____ (adj) is helpful because it is easy.

10. When you _____ (v) one thing with another, you mix them together.

B Work with a partner. Replace the crossed-out word with the correct adjective, noun, or verb form. Use a dictionary if necessary.

1. This restaurant serves a delicious ~~combine~~ _____ of Thai and Japanese food.

2. Although the ~~advise~~ _____ that she gave him was excellent, he ignored it.

3. It's ~~convenience~~ _____ to live close to a subway station, but it's also noisy.

4. If you're feeling ~~illness~~ _____, find a doctor who can ~~treatment~~ _____ you.

5. If you want to eat better, I ~~suggestion~~ _____ that you talk to a ~~nutrition~~ _____.

C Write TWO short answers to each question. Then share your ideas with a partner.

1. For a cheap, delicious meal, where would you **advise** people to go?

    _____   _____

2. What two dishes do you think everyone should know a **recipe** for?

    _____   _____

3. What are two common but not serious **illnesses** that you know?

    _____   _____

4. What are two excellent **suggestions** you have received from friends?

    _____   _____

D **BRAINSTORM** Create word maps for the words in the ovals. Write words that will help you remember the meaning of each word. These could be words that are related to it or synonyms or antonyms of the word.

| Critical Thinking

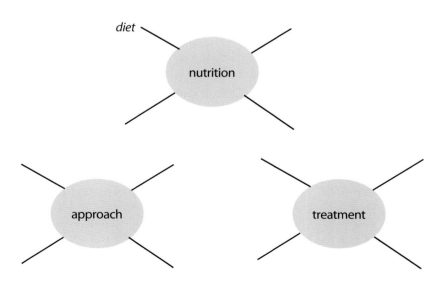

B Listening Culinary Medicine

Critical Thinking

A **PREDICT** You are going to hear a talk about culinary medicine. With a partner, discuss what you think "culinary medicine" means and what the talk might be about.

culinary (adj) /ˈkə-lə-nɛr-iʸ/ connected with food or cooking
medicine (n) /ˈme-dɪ-sən/ the treatment of health issues, such as illness

NOTE-TAKING SKILL   Divide the Page into Parts

It's a good idea to organize your notes as you take them. This makes it easier to review your notes later. One approach is to divide the page into parts and take notes about different things in each part. For example, you could draw a line down the middle of a page and note main ideas and/or problems on the left side and details and/or solutions on the right side.

After listening, you may find it helpful to read through your notes and add questions you would like to ask or do research on.

B **MAIN IDEAS** Read notes about the talk and confirm your predictions from exercise A. Then watch or listen to the talk and choose the correct summary, a or b. 🔊 ▶

Culinary Medicine	
Main Ideas	**Details**
Culinary medicine (CM)	Combines food + cooking with medicine
Poor nutrition and diet cause health issues	People don't have time to cook healthy foods Convenient foods are low cost but usually not healthy

CM is solution to this problem	Educate people about
	  - how food affects health
	  - how to cook healthy food
	
	Doctor can give suggestions

Not all doctors are able to do this	Training doctors is a solution e.g., Doctors in the Kitchen program
Do it yourself if doctor can't help	Use websites like "Plant-Based Los Angeles" Cook healthy recipes using fruits, vegetables, nuts, etc.
Hard to change diet, but CM is good place to start	

a. The speaker contrasts culinary medicine with popular health care approaches. He discusses some issues with this approach and offers solutions to those problems. He gives examples of patients who have found culinary medicine helpful and those who have found it unhelpful. He concludes by saying that doctors and nutritionists should talk more.

b. The speaker explains what culinary medicine is and how it combines the approaches of doctors and nutritionists. He discusses issues with this approach and suggests ways to solve these problems. He gives some examples of people and places that are trying to introduce culinary medicine. He concludes by summarizing the main ideas of the talk.

C   DETAILS   Listen again. Answer each question with ONE word you hear. 🔊

1.   What food is cheap and convenient but not healthy? _____

2.   Where can families put cooked meals for a later time? _____

3.   In which country does the "Doctors in the Kitchen" program run? _____

4.   What can doctors who are trained in culinary medicine give to their patients? _____

5.   What is the main ingredient in the recipes of the doctor who started a website in the USA? _____

6.   What does this website include with the recipes? _____

LISTENING SKILL   **Listen for Problems and Solutions**

When discussing problems and solutions, speakers may discuss:
- One issue and then one solution at a time, OR
- All the issues and then all the solutions.

Pay attention to words and phrases that signal when a speaker is going to describe a problem or present a solution.

Problem: *A major problem is . . . / The issue is . . . / One concern is . . .*
Solution: *The solution is . . . / . . . offers a solution / Having . . . can help / What can you do? You can . . .*

D   Using the notes and your memory of the talk, check the way the speaker organizes the talk.

a.   _____ He discusses the issues and their solutions one after another.

b.   _____ He discusses all of the issues and then all of the solutions.

E   FOCUSED LISTENING   Listen to excerpts. In each one, does the speaker mention a problem, a solution, or both? Write P for *Problem*, S for *Solution*, or B for *Both*. 🔊

1.   _____

2.   _____

3.   _____

4.   _____

F   Look again at the notes. What questions would you like to ask or research about the talk?

B Speaking

Critical Thinking **A** **EXPLAIN** Work in a group. Ask each other for your opinions about the statements below.

1. Great recipes usually have simple ingredients and are easy to follow.
2. Children whose parents are good cooks usually become good cooks, too.
3. It is OK to eat anything you want as long as you don't eat too much of it.

PRONUNCIATION   Spelling Patterns for Long Vowel Sounds

🔊 Most vowel sounds in English can be spelled in different ways, but some spelling patterns are especially common.

The /e^y/ sound is often spelled *ai* (aid) or *ay* (day).

| *paid* | *tail* | *mail* | *stay* | *way* | *always* |

The /i^y/ sound is often spelled *ea* (eat) or *ee* (see).

| *appeal* | *meal* | *tea* | *three* | *seem* | *deep* |

The /a^y/ sound is often spelled *i* (kind) or *y* (style).

| *child* | *climb* | *blind* | *bye* | *type* | *rhyme* |

The /o^w/ sound is often spelled *oa* (road) or *ow* (below).

| *goal* | *loan* | *approach* | *throw* | *know* | *window* |

When the last three letters of a word are vowel + consonant + -e, the sound of the vowel *a*, *e*, *i*, and *o* is usually the sound of its name: /e^y/ for *a*, /i^y/ for *e*, and so on.

| *late* | *complete* | *fine* | *note* |

B Say the words and think about the sound of the letters in bold. Put the words in the correct columns. Then work with a partner to add additional words for each long vowel sound. These could be words that follow the common spelling patterns or words that use a different spelling pattern.

| ad**vi**se | f**ee**l | l**ow** | m**i**nd | r**ai**n | s**ea**son |
| ex**tre**me | g**oa**l | m**a**ke | p**ay** | r**oa**d | tr**y** |

/e^y/	/i^y/	/a^y/	/o^w/

Critical Thinking **C** **BRAINSTORM** Work in a group. You have three minutes to make a list of food names that have long vowel sounds. You will get one point for each long vowel sound in a word. So, for example, *cheese* would score one point, *ice cream* would score two, and *baked potato* would score three! Which group will win?

D **EVALUATE** What are some things people can do to make sure they eat well? Add TWO ideas to this list. Then check (✓) the FIVE ideas that you think would be the most useful for you. Share your choices with a partner. Pronounce the underlined vowels carefully. | Critical Thinking

1. ☐ M<u>a</u>ke a m<u>ea</u>l plan.
2. ☐ Purchase gr<u>o</u>cer<u>ie</u>s onl<u>i</u>ne.
3. ☐ Prepare food <u>o</u>ver the w<u>ee</u>kend for <u>ea</u>ting during the w<u>ee</u>k.
4. ☐ Bring food from h<u>o</u>me instead of <u>ea</u>ting out at luncht<u>i</u>me.
5. ☐ Gr<u>ow</u> your <u>ow</u>n vegetables.
6. ☐ <u>Ea</u>t wh<u>o</u>le foods, not processed ones.
7. ☐ Alw<u>ay</u>s have breakfast.
8. ☐ Before you <u>ea</u>t something, ask yourself: Am <u>I</u> hungry or just bored?

9. ☐ _____

10. ☐ _____

CRITICAL THINKING Prioritize

When you have to make decisions, it's important to evaluate what things or tasks are most important. This can help you to prioritize—decide which things to keep, action to take, or tasks to do first. Usually, the things we value, such as our health, working hard, and having positive relationships can help us to make these decisions.

E Work with a partner to discuss which THREE ideas from exercise D (or other ideas you can think of) would most help these people and why. | Critical Thinking

1. Jayna wants to eat healthily, but she's too busy at work to cook each day.
2. Antoine has a part-time job, so he doesn't have much money to spend on food.
3. Myeong-Jung can't cook very well, so she eats a lot of unhealthy take-out food.

Growing chili peppers at home

Review

A VOCABULARY Complete the tasks with the words in the box.

advise	apply	approach	combine	display	label	react	treatment

Categorize the words according to . . .

1. their part of speech: both nouns and verbs, nouns only, or verbs only.
2. their long vowel sound: /e^y/ as in *pay*, /i^y/ as in *see*, /a^y/ as in *lie*, or /o^w/ as in *below*.
3. how well you know them: know and can use, know, or need to study more.

B PRONUNCIATION Consider the vowel sounds in the underlined words. Which spelling patterns do they follow? Then say the sentences.

1. It is <u>time</u> for you to <u>shine</u>.
2. It is the <u>same</u> whole <u>grain</u>.
3. Wear your <u>own</u> <u>coat</u>.
4. Let's <u>eat</u> some <u>beets</u>.

C GRAMMAR Complete the paragraph by writing the verbs in parentheses in the correct voice: active or passive.

We should ¹_____ (remember) that advertisements for food

²_____ (design) to affect our behavior. In many cases, words, images, and

colors ³_____ (use) that make the food look delicious. The ad might also

⁴_____ (include) words that make the food sound natural and healthy. In some

ads, low prices ⁵_____ (mention) to make people want to purchase the food.

D SPEAKING SKILL Discuss these statements with a partner. Support your ideas.

1. It's important to understand food psychology.
2. The milkshake experiment is interesting.
3. All doctors should practice culinary medicine.

RE-ASSESS What skills or language still need improvement?

Final Tasks

OPTION 1 Discuss how grocery stores affect consumers

A **BRAINSTORM** Complete the tasks.

1. Think of specific examples of these ways that grocery stores affect the behavior of customers.
   - What kind of music customers hear
   - How the store is organized
   - Where the store puts products
   - What sales and deals are available

2. Brainstorm ways that customers can avoid being affected when grocery stores use food psychology.

B Work in a group. Using your ideas from exercise A, discuss your opinions about how grocery stores try to affect the behavior of their customers and how customers can avoid this.

> *I think stores know people are often in a hurry, so they display things in places they know everyone will see, such as by the entrance or by the check-out counters. Some stores even put displays in the middle of aisles to get people's attention since they have to walk around the displays. If the store can get people's attention, then they might be able to interest them enough to make a purchase.*

C After the discussion, consider these questions:
   - How do you feel about your participation in the group discussion?
   - Did you use the skills and language from this unit?

▼ Customers at a supermarket in Sweden

See Unit 4 Rubric in the Appendix.

OPTION 2 Debate whether cooking should be taught in schools

COLLABORATION SKILL   Participate in a Debate

In a debate, two teams discuss a statement or question. One team supports (agrees with) the statement. The other team opposes (disagrees with) it. In a debate, you may have to support an opinion you do not agree with personally.

During a debate, teams take turns speaking and cannot interrupt when it is the other team's turn. Some debates have three parts. First, each team presents their ideas. Then they have some time to prepare a response to the other team's ideas. Finally, they present their response. Another person or team will decide which team wins.

To debate well, speak clearly, give strong reasons, examples, and explanations for your ideas, and explain why you think the other team's ideas are less convincing than yours.

A MODEL Listen to a short debate. Complete the chart. 🔊

1. What is the topic of the debate?	
2. Do the speakers in Team A agree or disagree with the topic? What reasons do they give?	
3. Do the speakers in Team B agree or disagree with the topic? What reasons do they give?	

B ANALYZE THE MODEL Listen again. Discuss the questions with a partner. 🔊

1. Do both teams follow the rules of a debate?
2. Which team won the debate, in your opinion? Why?

C PLAN Work with a partner. Your teacher will tell you to support or oppose the statement below. Remember that this might not be your real opinion. Brainstorm ideas with reasons, details, and examples that support the opinion. Also, think about what your opponents might say so you will be ready to respond to their points.

> Cooking should be taught in school.

D PRACTICE With your partner, complete the tasks.

1. Choose the four best ideas from your list and decide who will say them during the debate.
2. Practice saying your ideas. Give each other feedback on how well you present your ideas.
3. Discuss ideas that the other team might mention. Think about how you can respond to them.

E DEBATE Form a group with a pair of students that were assigned the opposite opinion. Have the debate. Allow three minutes for each part: presenting, thinking about how to respond, and responding.

INSIDE THE BRAIN 5

KODAK READY-MOUNT

Catherine Panebianco preserves family memories by photographing old slides in her home.

IN THIS UNIT, YOU WILL:

- Listen to a group discussion about memory
- Watch a video on the brain
- Watch or listen to a podcast on how exercise benefits the brain
- Discuss strategies for learning another language **OR** Present advice to future students

THINK AND DISCUSS:

1. What memories does this room have for Catherine Panebianco?
2. How do you think Panebianco is related to the people at the table?
3. Do you have special memories of a room?

Read the information. Then discuss the questions.

1. Do any of the facts surprise you?

2. When might this information be useful? For example, if you are having a terrible day, you might tell yourself you're not likely to remember it tomorrow.

3. What would you like to learn about the brain?

Did You Know...?

There is a lot we know about the brain, but so much more that we don't. We know that there are billions of neurons (cells) in our brains making trillions of connections. These connections allow us to remember and learn information, among other things. However, scientists still have many questions, such as: How many different types of neurons are there? How do they communicate with each other? And how do all the parts of the brain work together? As scientists work to answer these questions, consider these amazing facts that we *do* know.

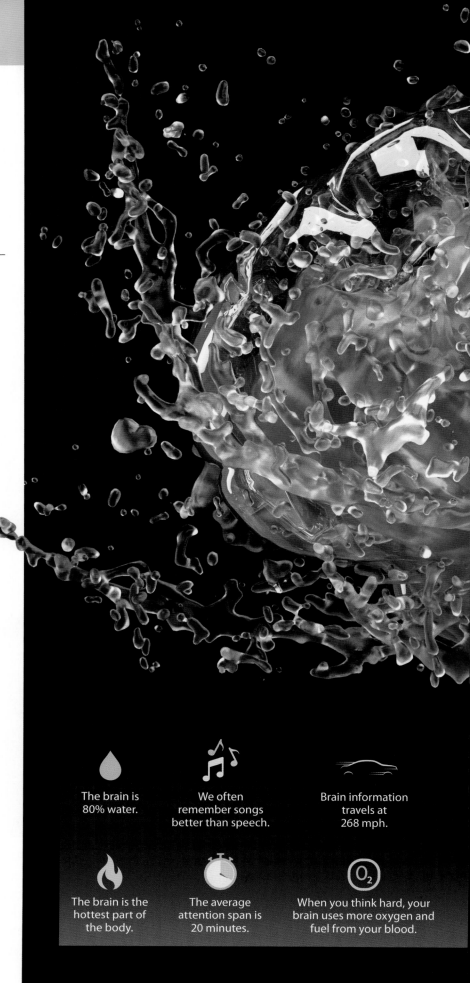

The brain is 80% water.

We often remember songs better than speech.

Brain information travels at 268 mph.

The brain is the hottest part of the body.

The average attention span is 20 minutes.

When you think hard, your brain uses more oxygen and fuel from your blood.

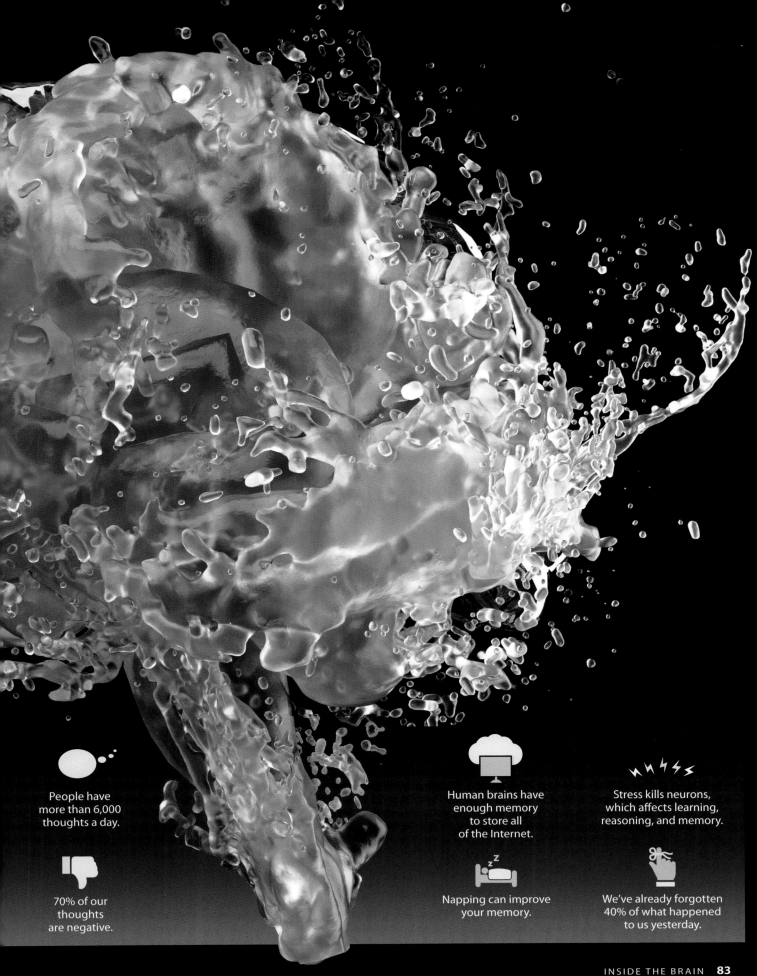

People have more than 6,000 thoughts a day.

70% of our thoughts are negative.

Human brains have enough memory to store all of the Internet.

Napping can improve your memory.

Stress kills neurons, which affects learning, reasoning, and memory.

We've already forgotten 40% of what happened to us yesterday.

A Vocabulary

A Listen and repeat. Check the words you know. 🔊

connection (n)	**long-term** (adj)	**normally** (adv)	**process** (n)	**store** (v)
function (v)	**loss** (n)	**permanently** (adv)	**short-term** (adj)	**wire** (n)

B **MEANING FROM CONTEXT** Listen and write the words you hear. Then think about each word's meaning. 🔊

THE MEMORY PROCESS

The memory [1]_____ involves several steps. First, you get some information from the environment. For example, you see or hear something. Next, that information goes into your sensory memory for a very short time. Third, information you pay attention to moves to your [2]_____ memory. Fourth, through repetition, the information moves into your [3]_____ memory. You may remember some information [4]_____—for your whole life— once it gets [5]_____ in your long-term memory. When you repeat the information, you strengthen the [6]_____ between neurons, which play an important role in memory. Neurons [7]_____ like [8]_____ that send messages throughout your body. If you can make connections between neurons stronger or create new connections, you are more likely to remember information. Information [9]_____ is also part of a [10]_____ functioning memory. Any information that doesn't move from sensory memory to short-term memory or from short-term memory to long-term memory is lost.

Attention   Repetition

Sensory memory → Short-term memory → Long-term memory

Recall/use

Information loss   Information loss

C Complete the sentences with the correct form of the words from exercise A.

1. They have a _____ relationship. They've been married for 29 years.

2. Your brain and body cannot _____ well if you do not eat and sleep enough.

3. He got a(n) _____ job in an office. It's only for six weeks.

4. I keep my personal information on my desktop, and I _____ everything for work on the laptop I got from the company.

5. The storm caused some _____ to come down. Be careful not to touch them in case they are still carrying electricity.

6. How can I _____ delete these photos from my phone? I don't want them anymore.

7. There is a _____ between losing sleep and memory _____. When you don't get enough sleep, you can't remember and learn things as well as when you are rested.

8. The college application _____ takes several months. There are many steps to complete, such as choosing colleges to apply to, completing each application, and taking a standardized test.

9. The washing machine isn't working _____. I'm not sure what's wrong with it.

D Make collocations with the words in bold. Complete the sentences with the correct form of a word from the box.

close	function	permanently	short-term
crossed	loss	process	store

1. This is only a _____ **solution**.

2. Sadly, there was significant _____ **of life**.

3. The city is trying to _____ **eliminate** pollution.

4. Our TV does not _____ **properly** anymore.

5. My sister and I **have** a _____ **connection**; we are best friends.

6. We **got** our **wires** _____ and did not meet up.

7. The change of seasons is a **natural** _____.

8. All of the company's files are _____ **electronically** now; we don't keep paper files.

A Listening Making Memories

A **PREDICT** You are going to hear three students discuss three topics from their class notes about memories. Discuss these questions.

1. What are three topics about memory that the students might discuss?

2. How do you think the conversation will be organized?
   a. One person will discuss all the topics.
   b. Each person will discuss one topic.
   c. Two people will talk, and one will take notes.

3. Besides summarizing their notes, what else might the students say?

NOTE-TAKING SKILL **Organize Notes by Speaker or Topic**

Usually during a group or panel discussion, each person talks about a different topic or aspect of a topic. When you take notes:

- Organize your notes by speaker or topic.
- Divide your paper into sections for each person or topic.

Listening for how speakers signal turns can help you organize your notes. Here are some phrases to listen for.

Taking a turn	**Suggestion to take a turn**
I'll start/go first.	*Maybe you could start/go first.*
That ties in nicely with my topic.	*That leads into your topic.*
I guess it's my turn now.	*It looks like it's your turn now.*

B **MAIN IDEAS** Listen and take notes. Then answer the questions. 🔊

1. Which three topics about memory do the students discuss?
   a. how memory changes over time
   (b.) memory loss
   (c.) the memory process
   d. tips for improving memory
   (e.) two types of memories

2. Who discusses which topic? Write the letter of the topic next to the correct student.

   memory Process Liz   C

   explicit memory Julia   e

   _____ Toshi   b

   memory loss

Taking a wedding photo
in Shaghai, China

C DETAILS Listen again. Write T for *True* or F for *False*. 🔊

1. ___F___ Not everyone thought studying in the group was helpful.

2. ___T___ Important information moves from short-term memory to long-term memory.

3. ___F___ Memories become weaker when they travel down the same pathways in the brain.

4. ___T___ Explicit memories include information you think about a lot and repeat again
and again.

5. ___F___ Past experiences are examples of implicit memories.

6. ___T___ Memory loss is also called amnesia.

7. ___T___ Stress can cause amnesia.

8. ___F___ Amnesia can cause some permanent memory loss.
___T___

D FOCUSED LISTENING Listen to excerpts and write what you hear. What does each phrase
signal? 🔊

1. _____, Liz.

2. And Toshi, what you just said _____—two
types of memories: explicit and implicit memories.

3. All right, _____.

A Speaking

Critical Thinking | **A** **RECALL** Listening A was a study group discussion about memory. Discuss these questions.

1. What kinds of information can you remember easily (e.g., people's names, the words to songs, passwords)?
2. What is one of your earliest memories?
3. Why do you think people sometimes remember the same things differently?

Critical Thinking | **B** **RATE** Read the questionnaire. Decide how strongly you agree or disagree with each statement (1 = strongly disagree; 5 = strongly agree). Discuss your answers.

QUESTIONNAIRE: What helps you learn and remember?

1. It was easier to learn something new when I was younger.	1 2 3 4 ⑤
2. Even with practice, there are some things I can't learn how to do.	1 2 ③ ④ 5
3. I learn from mistakes more quickly than I learn in other ways.	1 2 3 ④ 5
4. It's easier for me to remember information if I write it down.	1 2 3 4 ⑤
5. It's easier for me to learn something new if someone shows me rather than tells me how to do it.	1 2 3 4 ⑤

See Speaking Phrases in the Appendix.

SPEAKING SKILL   Make Suggestions

When you make suggestions, you want them to sound polite and not too forceful. One way to do this is by using the modals *could, should,* and *might*.

> You **could** ask some classmates to form a study group.
> Maybe we **should** practice our presentation again before class.
> You **might** want to take the exam again.

Here are some other words and phrases you can use to make suggestions:

> **Let's** take a break.   **It's a good idea** to review your class notes.
> **Why don't you** take a break?   **It's helpful** to review your class notes.
> **I suggest** we take a break.

C With a partner, take turns asking for suggestions.

What's the best way to . . . ?

- become famous
- find a job
- save money
- learn to play an instrument

- pass a job interview
- meet new people
- learn how to cook
- relax

D APPLY Work with a partner. Read the strategies for how to improve memory or learning. Then make suggestions for the students below.

Critical Thinking

1
- Study new information within 24 hours

2
- Use letter or word patterns/associations

3
- Review information frequently (spaced studying)

4
- Repeat information you need to remember

5
- Connect new to old information

6
- Teach someone else

7
- Use visuals (note cards, concept maps)

8
- Get good sleep

1. Sami has a history test next week. 4, 5, 8
2. Paola wants to remember the names of her new classmates. 2
3. Omar is having a hard time remembering all the vocabulary for anatomy class. 5, 2, 7
4. Anh needs to memorize a presentation for work. 1, 7, 6

E SYNTHESIZE Look at the photo and read the caption. Then discuss the questions with a small group.

Critical Thinking

1. How are these students learning to cook?
2. What type of memory are the students' making: an explicit or implicit one?
3. A *risk* is the possibility of something bad happening. How is risk a part of learning?

▼ Using superheated woks, students at Shandong Lanxiang Senior Technical School learn how to stir-fry.

See Verbs
Followed by
Gerunds or
Infinitives in
the Appendix.

GRAMMAR FOR SPEAKING   Infinitives after Verbs

We use infinitives (*to* + base verb) after certain verbs. Notice the two patterns.

Verbs + infinitive

agree	continue	forget	plan	remember
begin	decide	learn	pretend	try

*My son is learning **to ride** a bicycle. He plans **to practice** every day.*
*I forgot **to bring** my notebook to class. Did you remember **to bring** yours?*

Verbs + object + infinitive

cause	inspire	remind	teach	warn
encourage	instruct	require	tell	

*Stress caused Dave **to have** memory problems.*
*Please remind me **to order** the birthday cake today.*

Some verbs can be used in either pattern, with different meanings.

ask	expect	help	like	promise
choose	get	hope	need	want

*I expect **to get** a good grade.*
*I expect you **to get** a good grade.*

F Complete each sentence with an appropriate infinitive.

1. I promise not _to spend_ too much money on my vacation.
2. Pablo tried _to help_ his friend John with his homework.
3. My daughter sometimes forgets _to brush_ her teeth in the morning.
4. When Mehmet wants _to learn_ a new vocabulary word, he writes it down.
5. Did the Nortons decide not _to buy_ a new car?
6. Lee needs ~~to me to go with~~ after class today. to eat
7. Do you plan _to ~~put~~, take_ another English class next semester?
8. I really hope _to go to_ London someday.
9. My parents always encouraged me _to do_ my best.
10. The teacher warned us not _to ~~come~~_ late for class. arriv, be

G With a partner, take turns finishing these sentences with infinitives.

1. When I was a child, I wanted . . .
2. Next year, I plan . . .
3. In this class, I'm learning . . .
4. I really hope . . .
5. Yesterday, I forgot . . .
6. I've decided . . .

3-D Brain Scans

unconventional (adj) unusual
gap (n) an empty space

something you can see

manifestation (n) a symptom or sign
keep track of (v phr) to know where something is

▲ Dr. Lichtman at his lab at
Harvard University

A Watch the video. Complete the summary with words you hear. ▶

Dr. Lichtman believes that there's a lot we don't know about how the brain works

because we need to see the ¹_____wires_____. He and others are working

to understand how cells in the brain ²_____communicate_____ with each other. They create 3-D

images of brain cells, and that allows them to see all the ³_____colors_____ of every cell

generate

connection

in one area.

B Watch again. Write T for *True* and F for *False*. ▶

1. __T__ Dr. Lichtman compares complete knowledge of the brain to one mile.

2. __F__ Students thought we had learned very little of everything we need to know about
the brain.

3. __F__ We have a clear idea of what brains are made up of.

4. __T__ In a large number of nervous system diseases, nothing appears wrong with the brain.

5. __F__ The colors Dr. Lichtman and his team use in their diagrams have special meanings.

6. __T__ Dr. Lichtman believes that knowledge can make you realize what you don't know.

C **EXPLAIN** Discuss why you think it's important to study the brain. | Critical Thinking

Vocabulary

A Listen and repeat. Check the words you know. 🔊

chemical (n)	**function** (n)	**mood** (n)	**signal** (n)	**structure** (n)
complex (adj)	**generate** (v)	**perform** (v)	**speed** (n)	**tiny** (adj)

B **MEANING FROM CONTEXT** Listen and write the words you hear. Then think about each word's meaning. 🔊

FACTS ABOUT YOUR BRAIN

1. Your brain is an extremely _Complex_ organ. It contains over 100 billion neurons that are constantly sending messages. Different neurons send messages at different _speed_ —some faster and some slower.

2. When you exercise, your brain produces a _chemical_ that makes it easier to learn. So, if you're having trouble with your homework, taking a break to do something active might be a good idea.

3. The common belief that we use only a _tiny_ amount (10 percent) of our brains is wrong. Each part of the brain has a _function_ , so we use 100 percent of our brains.

4. Even without words, you can figure out how someone is feeling. A part of your brain called the amygdala lets you "read" other people's faces and understand what kind of _mood_ they are in.

5. Every time you think, laugh, or sneeze, chemical and electrical _signals_ are moving between neurons. These messages make it possible for your brain to communicate with your body.

6. Learning changes the _structure_ of the brain. When you learn a new skill, such as playing a musical instrument, your brain cells organize themselves in a new way.

7. Your brain is extremely powerful. When you're awake, it _generate_ between 10 and 23 watts of electricity—enough to power a light bulb.

8. Your brain accesses and reacts to information incredibly quickly. It _perform_ faster than a supercomputer.

C Choose the correct word to complete each sentence.

1. Your brain produces **chemicals** that make you feel happy. These (<u>substances</u> / cells) are dopamine, serotonin, oxytocin, and endorphins.

2. Brainstorming is a good way to **generate** ideas. You can (get / <u>get rid of</u>) ideas that way.

3. When you're riding a bicycle, it's important to use hand **signals**. They allow you to (<u>control</u> / communicate with) other people on the road.

4. My country has a **complex** history. There were (a few / <u>many</u>) people and events that made my country what it is today.

5. The **speed** of your Internet connection can affect how (<u>quickly</u> / safely) you can work online.

6. The pineal gland is a **tiny** organ located inside your brain. It is one of the (<u>smallest</u> / largest) organs in the human body.

7. An example of **performing** a task is (<u>responding to</u> / avoiding) an email.

8. Your bones and (height / <u>muscles</u>) are important parts of your body's **structure**.

9. Your **mood** is how you (think / <u>feel</u>) at a particular time.

10. The largest part of the human brain is the cerebrum. Its **functions** or (<u>jobs</u> / abilities) include controlling thought and movement.

VOCABULARY SKILL **Words with Multiple Meanings**

Some words have more than one meaning. The meanings may be similar but not exactly the same. Use the context to help you understand the different meanings.

> You should **store** important documents in the cloud, not on your desktop. (v = to keep information on a computer)
> Where do you **store** your suitcase when you're not traveling? (v = to put someplace for later use)

D Choose the best meaning for the words in bold. Use context clues to help.

generate a. (v) to cause to happen or exist; b. (v) to produce energy, especially electricity; c. (v) to produce a large quantity

1. ___b___ You can **generate** static electricity when you drag your feet across a rug.

2. ___c___ Humans **generate** tons and tons of plastic waste every year.

3. ___c___ The team meeting **generated** some good ideas.

function a. (n) ways of working; b. (n) a large or formal event; c. (n) part of a computer program

4. ___b___ The science department has several **functions** every year.

5. ___c___ The programmer couldn't get one **function** to work correctly.

6. ___a___ The human brain has many different **functions**.

Listening The Exercise-Brain Connection

Critical Thinking

A PREDICT You are going to hear a podcast about the effects of exercise on the brain. Discuss these questions with a partner.

1. What positive effects do you think exercise has on the brain?
2. Who do you think will talk more about the exercise-brain connection: the host or the guest?

B MAIN IDEAS Watch or listen and answer the questions. 🔊 ▶

1. According to the podcast, which TWO positive effects does exercise have on the brain?
   a. It helps reduce stress.
   b. It makes your brain larger.
   c. It improves your mood.
   d. It makes you smarter.

2. How does exercise help you to learn?
   a. It changes your brain structure.
   b. It makes your heart beat faster.
   c. It produces an important chemical.

3. According to the podcast, what are TWO things involved in learning?
   a. chemical and electrical signals
   b. mood
   c. neurons connecting
   d. practice

C DETAILS Listen again. Write T for *True* or F for *False*. 🔊

1. ___F___ Aaron is the expert on the brain.

2. ___T___ BDNF is the chemical that is produced when you exercise.

3. ___F___ Neurons move electrical and chemical signals around your body. *brain*

4. ___T___ When neurons get the same message from the brain again and again, it makes their connections stronger.

5. ___F___ You can get BDNF from your doctor.

▼ Mountain biking in Sedona, Arizona

LISTENING SKILL   Listen for Reasons and Explanations

The reasons and explanations a speaker gives for their ideas helps you to understand and evaluate the ideas.

Listen for these signal phrases speakers use before a reason or an explanation:

The reason for this . . .   *Let me explain.*   *That's/It's because . . .*
I study in the morning. **That's because** *my mind functions best then.*

Listen for these words after a reason:

This/That is how/why . . .   *. . ., so*
My mind functions best in the morning. **That's why** *I study then.*

D   Listen to excerpts from the podcast. Connect the ideas to the correct reason or explanation. 🔊

1. Your daily workout can make you smarter because ___c___

2. You have thoughts or perform actions because ___a___

3. Practicing something helps you learn because ___b___

4. BDNF helps neurons connect, so ___d___

a. chemical and electrical signals move throughout your body.

b. it helps forms connections between neurons.

c. after exercise, your body produces a chemical that helps you learn.

d. this is how it makes it easier for us to learn.

PRONUNCIATION   Recognize Linking

will i be handsome

🔊 In English, speakers do not usually pronounce each word separately. They join, or *link*, words together. Learning to recognize linking will help you understand what you hear. Here are two common types of linking.

Consonant sounds to vowel sounds

It's amazing! (It sounds like the /s/ moves to the beginning of *amazing*.)

Consonant sound to same consonant sound

He learns something new every day. (The /s/ is said a little longer.)

E   Listen and complete the sentences from the podcast with the linked words you hear. 🔊

1. Our ___guest today___ is Jocelyn Taylor.

2. You probably know that your brain ___generates some___ electricity.

3. But the ___brain is not an___ electrical device.

4. BDNF helps neurons connect, so ___this is___ how it makes it easier for us to learn—to bring this back to my earlier point.

F   **INFER** Work with a partner. Listen and answer the question. How might Aaron expect to get BNDF from a doctor? 🔊

| Critical Thinking

B Speaking

Walk   Work

Critical Thinking **A APPLY** Listening B was about how exercise can improve our ability to learn. In a small group, discuss how these groups of people might use the information in the podcast.

| employers | parents | students | teachers |

B PERSONALIZE Work with a small group. Read the information below. Then discuss what experiences you have had with group work or group projects.

> Research has shown that working in a group on a complex task can improve students' learning for several reasons. One reason is that they share the information they need to complete the task, and another reason is that groups provide an essential social element. However, research has also shown that some individuals remember less when they work in a group than when they work alone.

CRITICAL THINKING Evaluate Pros and Cons

It can be helpful to think about the pros (positive aspects) and cons (negative aspects) of a topic to understand it better. Sometimes we may see only the pros or cons of something, but trying to see the other side can help us gain a new perspective. *electric*

At first I could only see the negative aspects of an e-reader: the light from the screen and not being able to turn real pages. But then I considered how much easier it is to take out books from the library with an e-reader. That one positive aspect made me decide to buy one.

Critical Thinking **C** With your partner, brainstorm a list of benefits and possible problems with group projects. Write your ideas in the T-chart. Are you more or less willing to do a group project now?

Group Projects at School/Work	
(+) Pros	**(-) Cons**
more people = more ideas	some people don't do any work
work together can reduce stres	communicate with your group
You can learning from you group	Time management

D **APPLY** Work in a group. Decide which tasks would be better to do in a group or alone.
Critical Thinking

1. Brainstorming ideas for a research project *group*
2. Doing research *group*
3. Organizing ideas from research into a presentation *group*
4. Editing a presentation *group* *alone*
5. Practicing a presentation *alone* *group*

E **SYNTHESIZE** With the same group, decide on rules for group work. Write down the top five rules. Practice using infinitives and language for making suggestions.
Critical Thinking

> *Everyone needs to participate.*
> *The work should be divided equally.*

1. _____
2. _____
3. _____
4. _____
5. _____

Girls build robots at a secondary school in Oman.

Review

A **VOCABULARY** Check the words you can use.

chemical (n)	function (v)	mood (n)	process (n)	store (v)
complex (adj)	generate (v)	normally (adv)	short-term (adj)	structure (n)
connection (n)	long-term (adj)	perform (v)	signal (n)	tiny (adj)
function (n)	loss (n)	permanently (adv)	speed (n)	wire (n)

1. Look up any word you didn't check in a dictionary. Then write a sentence with the word.
2. Complete each question with a word from the unit.

   a. What is the _____ between memory and learning?

   b. How do you approach a _____ task at school?

   c. How do you _____ ideas for a writing assignment?

B **PRONUNCIATION** Underline the words that you expect to be linked. Then say the sentences.

1. We can trick our brains in many ways.
2. There are different types of memories.
3. I have a good short-term memory.
4. My brain doesn't function in the morning.

C **GRAMMAR** Say sentences with infinitives or object + infinitives.

1. I want . . .   2. I encourage . . .   3. You should always try . . .   4. Let's agree . . .

D **SPEAKING SKILL** Give suggestions for each situation.

1. A: I have a new job, and it's hard for me to remember the names of my new coworkers.
   B: . . .

2. A: I want to learn another language, but I don't have time to take classes because of work.
   B: . . .

RE-ASSESS What skills or language still need improvement?

Final Tasks

OPTION 1 Discuss strategies for learning a language

A **BRAINSTORM** List some strategies that have helped you learn English. Think about the following categories:

- Vocabulary
- Grammar
- Skills

B Work in a small group. Use your notes from exercise A to discuss the best strategies for learning another language. As you discuss, consider the following:

- What strategies does everyone use that are similar?
- What strategies do you or other people use that are different from everyone else?
- What strategies worked for someone else but not for you?
- What strategies do you want to try?

▼ Scientists research what changes take place in the brain during language learning and how a language can be learned most effectively.

OPTION 2 Present advice to future students

PRESENTATION SKILL   Describe Images

Images or visuals are effective ways to express a message and engage your audience. Sometimes you may want to describe an image to clarify why you are using it. Use the simple present or present continuous to describe an image.

This is a photo of a stack of notebooks. The notebooks are the kind that you write in with a pen or pencil, not the digital kind. Learning English is a complex process, and writing things down helps me to remember information better.

🛜 **ONLINE** To share an image during a video meeting or when you are giving a presentation online, you will need to share your screen. It's important not to share the screen the whole time. During your introduction and closing, stop sharing and talk to the camera directly.

A **MODEL** Listen to someone present a meme that gives advice to future students of this class. Complete the chart. 🔊

What is the picture of?	
What does the text say?	
How does the advice relate to learning?	

B **ANALYZE THE MODEL** Listen again and write what you hear. With a partner, identify the vocabulary or grammar from the unit and any phrases for making suggestions. 🔊

1. And the text says, "You _____ buy a lot of these."

2. . . . our teacher _____ several different notebooks.

3. Learning English is a _____ . . .

4. Some students may not want to have so many notebooks,
   but I _____ they have at least two.

C **PLAN** Use the chart from exercise A to create your meme.

D **PRACTICE AND PRESENT** Practice presenting your meme to a partner before you present it to the class.

KNOWLEDGE IS POWER 6

Self-taught artist Jasenko Đorđević, from Bosnia and Herzegovina, carving Superman into pencil lead

IN THIS UNIT, YOU WILL:

- Watch or listen to a podcast about teaching yourself
- Watch a video on a self-taught programmer
- Listen to a conversation about choosing a major
- Discuss sayings about education
  OR Present on something you want to study

THINK AND DISCUSS:

Đorđević creates tiny sculptures on pencils. He believes that people can also be reshaped throughout our lives.

1. How long do you think it took Đorđević to learn how to make pencil sculptures?

2. How does Djordjevic's knowledge make him powerful?

EXPLORE THE THEME

Look at the information. Then answer the questions.

1. What famous people do you know who you think might be multipotentialites?
2. What are some of your current interests?
3. John Urschel says that often "people want to divide the world into two," and don't consider that an athlete could also be a mathematician. How true do you think this is? Why?

$$= S_h^{v_2} \left(I_h - I_H^h L_H^{-1} \right.$$

$$\left. \frac{2\pi n x}{p} \right) + b_n \sin\left(\frac{2\pi n x}{p} \right)$$

Multipotentialites

Potential means a person's ability to develop or achieve. A multipotentialite is someone who has potential in many areas. He or she is interested in and does many things.

Multipotentialites are out-of-the-box thinkers who are especially good at solving complex problems. This is because they can learn quickly, adapt, combine ideas, see the big picture, and relate to different types of people.

John Urschel balanced playing professional football in the United States and studying math at an advanced level at the Massachusetts Institute of Technology (MIT), a top university in the USA. In his book about his life, he writes, "So often, people want to divide the world into two [. . .] Athlete and mathematician. Why can't something (or someone) be both?"

$$\| I -$$

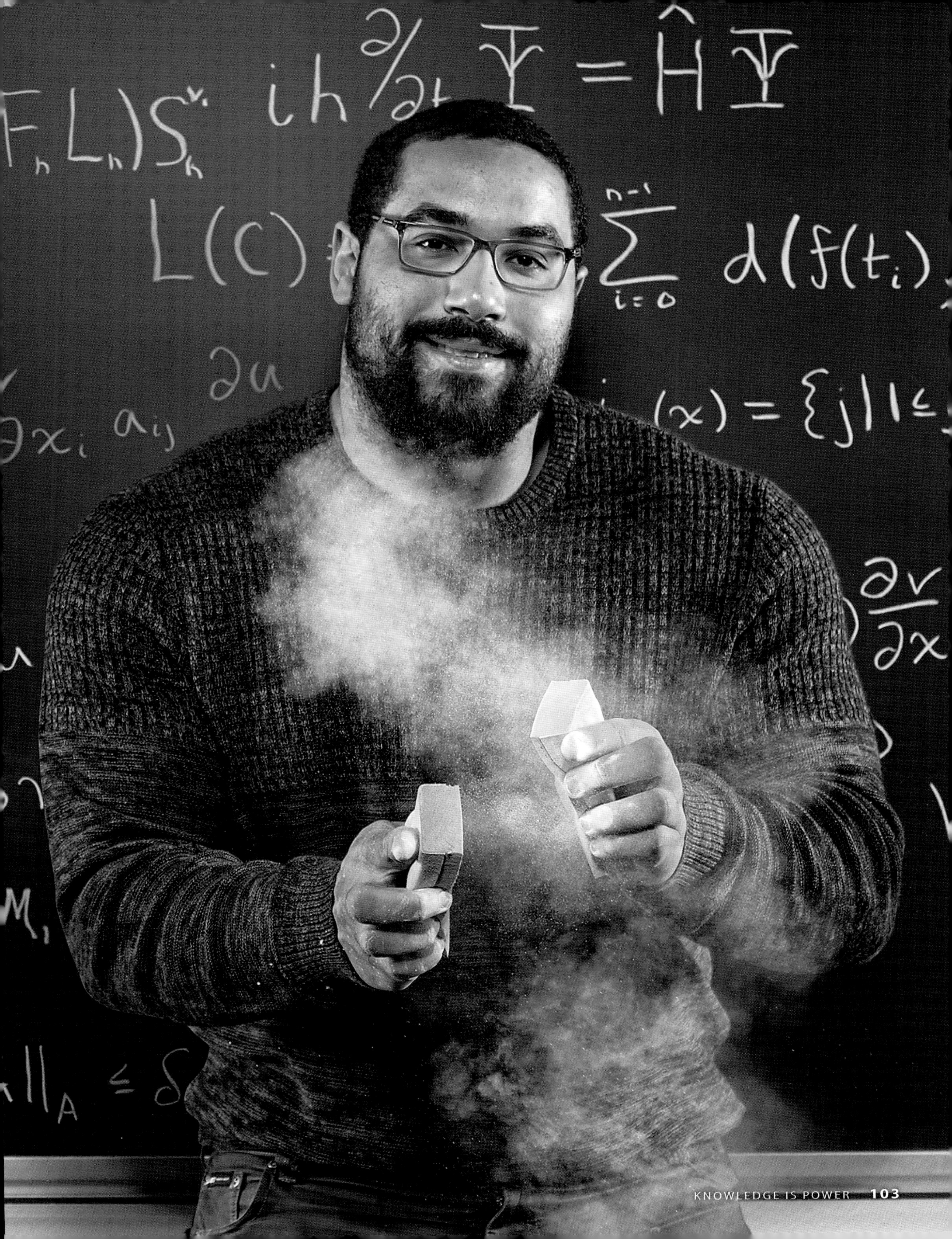

A Vocabulary

A **MEANING FROM CONTEXT** Listen and notice the words in blue. Think about the meaning of each word and then complete the definitions with the words. 🔊

THE FEYNMAN TECHNIQUE

Richard Feynman is one of the most important scientists of the last 100 years. He attended MIT and Princeton University, two of the best colleges in the United States, and then became a professor. During his life, he developed several major ideas that helped him **gain** fame, **success**, and even a Nobel Prize. Feynman was also known as an excellent teacher.

Even if you know little about the history of science, you may be **familiar** with Feynman's name from the so-called "Feynman **Technique**." This is an **effective** way to learn something quickly. The method is similar to an old saying: If you want to learn something well, teach it to others. Feynman went further. He said you only know something well if you can explain it in a simple way so that even children can understand. This **ability** is one that many great teachers have.

The Feynman Technique has several stages. First, choose a topic you feel is **worth** knowing. Second, find and study useful **resources** for learning about this topic. After that, explain what you have learned to a child. Doing this will help you recognize things that you need to study more because your **knowledge** of the topic is not complete. You will also recognize things the child did not understand. This could be because your explanation was too hard, or perhaps some of what you said was not **relevant**. Finally, go back to stage two and repeat the process. Keep doing this until you feel you understand the topic completely and can explain it simply.

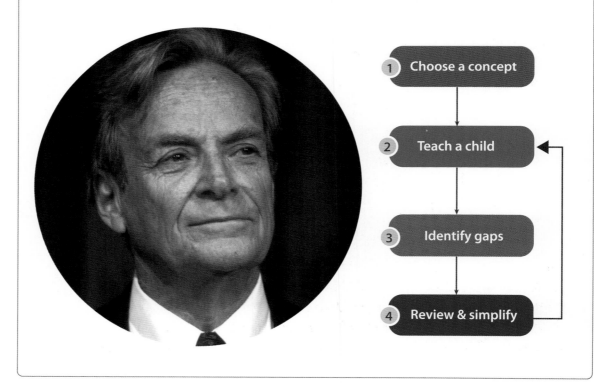

1. Choose a concept

2. Teach a child

3. Identify gaps

4. Review & simplify

1. _knowledge_ (n) are things that support learning or working. _resources_

2. _knowledge_ (n) is information that comes from learning or experience.

3. A(n) _technical_ _familiar_ (adj) person or thing is well-known or easy to recognize.

4. A(n) _technique_ (n) is a special or particular way of doing something.

5. A(n) _ability_ (n) is something that a person can do well, such as a skill.

6. If something is _worth_ (adj) knowing, it is important or useful.

7. Something _relevant_ (adj) is connected to or useful for a situation or person.

8. Something _effective_ (adj) works well and produces positive results or effects.

9. To achieve _success_ (n) means to achieve a goal or other positive result.

10. To _gain_ (v) something means to get it.

B Work with a partner to complete the word form chart. Use a dictionary if necessary.

	Noun	Verb	Adjective
1.	ability	– – – – – – –	~~familiar~~ able
2.	~~resources~~ gain	gain	– – – – – – –
3.	knowledge	to know	~~effective~~ knowledgable
4.	~~success~~ ~~technique~~ relevance	– – – – – – –	relevant
5.	success	succeed	~~worth~~ successful

C Complete the sentences with the correct word from the chart in exercise B.

1. Many people hope to _gain_ success in their life, especially through their job.

2. It can sometimes be hard to understand the _relevance_ of information you learn in school.

3. Richard Feynman was a very _successful_ scientist from the United States.

4. If I'm _able_ to take extra courses each semester, I can graduate early.

5. My mother is a _knowledgable_ person. I can ask her anything and she has a good answer.

D **PERSONALIZE** Work with a group to discuss the questions.

1. What is one **technique** you find especially valuable for studying?
2. What is a useful **ability** that you have developed recently?
3. Do you prefer to **gain knowledge** by reading, watching videos, or some other method?
4. Which is more useful for achieving **success** at work: being popular or being **effective?**

Listening Teaching Yourself

Critical Thinking

A ACTIVATE You are going to listen to a podcast about teaching yourself. Think about two things you have taught yourself. Then discuss these questions with a partner.

1. How well did you learn the things you taught yourself?
2. Why didn't you study these things with a teacher?

LISTENING SKILL Recognize Transitions

Transitions are changes from one idea or point to another. Speakers may signal transitions in different ways:

1. Sequence words
   First, I'll explain the issue, which is . . . OK, **next,** I'll discuss some solutions.

2. Direct references to previous and new points or ideas
   OK, that was the **second point**. Now let's **move on** and discuss . . .

3. Rhetorical questions and indirect questions
   OK, so **what can we do about this?** Well, there are several things.
   You might ask **why this is a problem**. There are two main reasons.

B MAIN IDEAS Watch or listen and number the ideas in the order the speaker discusses them. TWO ideas are extra. 🔊 ▶

a. _____ How to be an effective autodidact

b. _4_ What the cons of being an autodidact are

c. _3_ What the pros of being an autodidact are

d. _1_ What the meaning of *autodidact* is

e. _____ Which resources are good for autodidacts

f. _2_ Why people want to become autodidacts

A young girl learns to play a piano with educational stickers on the keys.

C **DETAILS** Listen again and take notes. Write short answers for each question. 🔊

1. In addition to learning how to do podcasts, what did the speaker teach herself?

   to be a translator, several languages

2. Who does the speaker say are examples of autodidacts?

   The tennis coach, Richard williams

3. What is the most common reason people become autodidacts?

   People want to learn something there are interested in

4. What is the main advantage of being an autodidact?

   it's cheep or free

5. What can it be hard to do without a teacher?

   it has to push yourself

6. What is a problem with relying on the Internet to get information?

   there is lot of mistakes of the internet, not all resources are good

D **DETAILS** Use your notes to check the benefits of being an autodidact that the speaker mentions. TWO ideas are not mentioned.

a. ✓ You become better at thinking critically.

b. ✓ You do not have to spend a lot of money.

c. _____ You learn at the speed that's right for you.

d. _____ You will learn how to learn effectively.

e. ✓ You study only when it's convenient for you.

E **BRAINSTORM** Work with a group to discuss other benefits of teaching yourself things. Consider the social and emotional aspects of learning, as well as the knowledge and experience you can gain.

Critical Thinking

F **RANK** If you have a lot of interests in addition to responsibilities like school and work, you need to manage your time. Put the time management tips in order from most to least helpful for you (1 = most helpful). Then share your ranking with a partner.

Critical Thinking

_____ Accept that you don't need to be an expert in everything.

_____ Combine your interests if you can.

_____ Don't get distracted by your phone.

_____ Have a morning routine.

_____ Organize your time by hours in a week.

_____ Take breaks when you need them.

A Speaking

See Irregular Comparatives and Superlatives in the Appendix.

GRAMMAR FOR SPEAKING   Comparative and Superlative Adjectives

---

We use comparative and superlative adjectives to compare people or things.

	Adjective	Comparative (+ *than*)	Superlative
one syllable	hard	harder	the hardest
two syllables ending in -*y*	funny easy	funnier easier	the funniest the easiest
two or more syllables	successful common	more/less successful more/less common	the most/least successful the most/least common
two-syllables with two forms	friendly quiet	friendlier/more friendly quieter/more quiet	the friendliest/the most friendly the quietest/the most quiet

> The library is a **quieter** place to study **than** my room.
> Math is **the hardest** of my classes.

With both comparatives and superlatives, the second part of the comparison can be a noun phrase.

> This week's test was **more difficult than** the one that we had last week.
> This week's test was probably **the hardest** one that we've had all year.

We can make comparative adjectives stronger by using *a lot, even, far,* and *much*. We can use *a bit* or *a little* to make a comparative adjective less strong.

> Today's test was **much harder than** our last one. I hope our next one is **a bit easier**.

A Read the sentences. Check the correct ones. Correct the ones with errors.

1. ☑ History textbooks can be much longer than textbooks used for other classes. ✓

2. ☑ The University of Bologna in northern Italy is one of the oldest in the world. ✓

3. ☐ Half the students failed the test because they thought it would be more easy. ~~much~~ easier

4. ☑ College students often study in the library because it is quieter than other places. ✓

5. ☑ Students stopped attending the class as it was ~~far~~ more boring than they had expected.

6. ☑ Many people think Seoul National University is the best one in South Korea. ✓

7. ☐ Courses at Canadian colleges are often cheap and short than courses at universities. cheaper shorter

8. ☑ Einstein and Feynman are two of the most famous and important scientists in history ✓

B Describe the photo on the next page using comparative and superlative adjectives. Use the words in the box below and your own ideas.

big	bright	colorful	dark	fun	pretty

The Barbie house and the all-black house in Santa Monica, CA, USA

C **PERSONALIZE** Work in a group. Take turns answering these questions.

1. What subjects do you think are the most interesting to study? The least interesting?
2. Who was the best teacher you had when you were younger? What made him or her the best?
3. In your view, what is the most important thing students can do to learn effectively?
4. What is the most interesting thing you have learned in this class so far?

CRITICAL THINKING Apply Previous Knowledge

When you learn something new, you can analyze, understand, and remember it more easily if you use your previous knowledge. This includes what you know from personal experience and what you have read or heard but not experienced.

Spend some time considering what you already know about

- the topic itself
- similar or related topics
- how the world works

If the new information seems very different from your previous knowledge about it, it's a good idea to check whether the new information is correct. This is especially true if the new information comes from a source you are not sure is reliable.

D Discuss what you know about learning English with a small group. Answer the questions.

Critical Thinking

1. How easy or difficult would it be for you to teach yourself English?
2. Why might it be easier for some people to teach themselves than for others?
3. Are some parts of learning English easier to learn on your own than others? (e.g., vocabulary, grammar, pronunciation)

🔊 Consonants are usually pronounced, but some words have silent consonants. Often, silent consonants are part of a sequence, or cluster, of consonants.

The *b* in *mb* and *bt* is always silent at the end of a word.

thumb /θʌm/   *doubt* /daʷt/

The *k* in *kn* is always silent at the beginning of a word.

know /noʷ/   *knife* /naʸf/

The *w* in *wr* is always silent at the beginning of a word.

write /raʸt/   *wrong* /rɔŋ/

E Complete the words with the correct two-letter clusters from the Pronunciation box. Then practice saying the words.

1. cli__mb__   5. _____ock   9. _____ot

2. _____ee   6. _____ote   10. la_____

3. _____ist   7. co_____   11. _____ew

4. _____ap   8. thu_____   12. de_____

F Work with a partner. Choose situation 1, 2, or 3. Underline all the silent consonants. Then decide who should be person A and person B and make up a conversation.

1. A: You're a climber. You hurt your wrist and thumb. Tell your doctor what happened.
   B: You're a doctor. A patient visits you. Ask questions and give the patient some advice.

2. A: You're a shopper at a store. You don't know where the combs are. Ask for help.
   B: You work at a store. A customer can't find something. Help the customer.

3. A: You're a student. You took a test but got many items wrong. Ask a teacher for help.
   B: You're a teacher. A student got many answers wrong on a test. Advise the student.

▼ Indoor climbing, Barcelona, Spain

The World's Oldest Programmer

Video

▲ Masako Wakamiya

A Watch the video. Check the THREE statements that describe main ideas. ▶

a. _____ Many elderly people in Japan find it hard to communicate with others.

b. _____ Masako wrote an app to help seniors become interested in technology.

c. _____ Because Masako uses her laptop often, making an app was easy for her.

d. _____ The app Masako created is a game based on Japanese traditional culture.

e. _____ Learning new things can help older people keep their brains healthy.

B Watch again. Complete the statements with ONE word or a number that you hear. ▶

1. Masako started using a laptop to be able to contact her _____.

2. She decided to program an app when she was _____ years old.

3. Compared with younger developers, Masako had more _____ about what older people would want.

4. Teaching ourselves new things has many _____ for older people.

5. According to the speaker, Masako's life began again at age _____.

C **PERSONALIZE** If you designed or programmed an app, would it be a game or something else? What would it be about? Who would find it interesting and why? Share your answers.

B Vocabulary

A **MEANING FROM CONTEXT** Read and listen to the information. Notice the words in blue and think about their meanings. 🔊

> ### COMMON STUDENT CONCERNS . . . DON'T LET THEM WORRY YOU!
>
> Going to college is a big step, so it's natural to have concerns. Your life is going to change in many ways, and you will face **challenges**. But you'll be able to **deal with** most issues if you work hard, get help from others, and look after your health.
>
> Some students believe they're not clever enough for college. They feel **intimidated** by how smart everyone else seems. If you have this feeling, talk to friends and classmates. You'll soon **realize** that many people think this way. Just remember that if you have been accepted to a college, you're definitely **bright** enough to be there. In other words, if you believe in yourself and do the work for your classes, you'll be fine.
>
> Choosing what to study can also cause stress. But you don't need to choose a major until the end of your second year, so there's plenty of time! And even if you think you know what you'll **major in**, it's a good idea to **check out** a variety of classes before you make your final decision. You may really **get into** something and **end up** choosing a major you'd never considered before. And if you really can't decide, don't forget that you probably have the **option** to major in one subject and minor in another.

B Complete the sentences with the words from exercise A.

1. Although his parents wanted it, the student did not _____ choosing economics as his major.

2. The student chose to _____ education so she could become a teacher.

3. Despite being _____, the student didn't study much and ended up doing badly on the test.

4. He wanted to study overseas, so the student decided to _____ universities in Australia.

5. Like many people, the successful scientist had to _____ issues when she was younger.

6. All the choices were good, so they decided on the cheapest _____.

7. I didn't like reading as a child, but I started to _____ it as an adult.

8. The speaker didn't _____ most of the information in his talk was unfamiliar to his audience.

9. The team overcame the _____ they faced after a lot of hard work.

10. You should never feel _____ about asking questions if you don't understand.

VOCABULARY SKILL   Phrasal Verbs

Phrasal verbs are verbs that go with a particle. A particle is a short word like *from, in, into, out,* or *up.*

>   He **filled out** the form.   She **comes from** Mexico.

Some phrasal verbs are "separable": the verb and particle can either be together or separated by an object. (If the object is a pronoun, they *must be* separated.)

>   He **filled out** <u>the form</u>. / He **filled** <u>the form</u> **out**.
>   He **filled** <u>it</u> **out**. / ~~He **filled out** it~~.

Other phrasal verbs are "inseparable": the verb and particle *cannot be* separated by the object.

>   She **comes from** <u>Mexico</u>. / ~~She **comes** Mexico **from**~~.

C   Add each phrasal verb from exercise B to the correct category.

Separable	Inseparable

D   Complete the tasks.

1. Find THREE more phrasal verbs in exercise A: one in the last sentence of each paragraph. Then add them to the chart in exercise C.

2. Complete the definitions of some common phrasal verbs. Then add the phrasal verbs to the chart in exercise C.

    a. _____ *on* : to go onto a bus, train, plane, or boat

    b. *wake* _____ : to stop sleeping or make someone else stop sleeping

    c. _____ *out* : to leave a place and go somewhere else

    d. *call* _____ : to return a person's telephone call

▼ A student studying late at the library

Listening Choosing a Major

Critical Thinking | **A** **ACTIVATE** Look at the chart and choose any FOUR of the majors. Then discuss the questions.

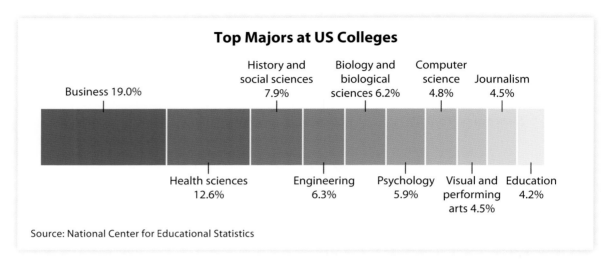

Top Majors at US Colleges

Business 19.0%

History and social sciences 7.9%

Biology and biological sciences 6.2%

Computer science 4.8%

Journalism 4.5%

Health sciences 12.6%

Engineering 6.3%

Psychology 5.9%

Visual and performing arts 4.5%

Education 4.2%

Source: National Center for Educational Statistics

1. Which of these majors are you familiar with? What do you know about them?
2. Why do you think these majors are popular? Are they popular in other places you know?
3. Which of the majors interest you and which do not? Why?

B **MAIN IDEAS** Listen to a conversation and answer the questions.

1. The speakers are probably
   a. a high schooler and her parent.
   b. a professor and college student.
   c. two friends who are students.

2. The speakers mainly discuss
   a. science as a possible option for the woman to major in.
   b. the pros and cons of having several options to major in.
   c. which science subjects the man recommends majoring in.

3. The woman will probably
   a. contact her professor to change her major.
   b. learn more about Mike Gil's science career.
   c. visit a website that the man recommended.

C **DETAILS** Listen again. Choose the correct answer.

1. How many majors is the man considering for next year?
   a. One   b. Two

2. What major does the woman say she would like to choose?
   a. Biology   b. History

3. What does the woman think about herself?
   a. She doesn't work hard enough.   b. She isn't smart enough.

4. How does the man react to what the woman says about herself?

    a. He's disappointed.   b. He's surprised.

5. Who started the SciAll.org website?

    a. Mike Gil   b. The man

6. What does the woman think about the man's suggestion?

    a. It might be helpful.   b. It sounds expensive.

D **FOCUSED LISTENING** Write what you think the short forms of these underlined words are. Then listen to the excerpts and confirm your ideas. Discuss other common short forms of words you know. 🔊

1. An <u>introduction</u> (___*intro*___) gives basic information about something.

2. A <u>professor</u> (_____) is a person who teaches classes at a college or university.

3. A <u>laboratory</u> (_____) is a place where students can do science experiments.

4. <u>Information</u> (_____) is facts about a person, a place, an event, and so on.

5. You can trust something <u>legitimate</u> (_____) because it is fair and honest.

E **PERSONALIZE** Discuss the questions with a group.

1. Do you think it is useful to hear from professionals about their career journey?

2. What questions would you have for Mike Gil?

3. Do you think you will check the SciAll.org website?

National Geographic
Explorer Dr. Mike Gil

Critical Thinking | **A RECALL** In Listening B, the speakers discussed SciAll.org. Discuss how you think that site would be useful to the groups below.

| junior high school students | first-year college students | high school science teachers |

B Read the information below. Label each section of the chart with the method of education—*at school*, *online*, *with a tutor*, or *by himself*.

Ahmed is a high school student. These days, he studies around 34 hours a week. He spends most of that time at school. Outside school, his focus is learning English: He sees a private tutor once a week for 90 minutes, takes a 60-minute online class three times a week, and teaches himself for about 30 minutes every day except Saturday and Sunday. He also spends two hours a week teaching himself how to play the guitar.

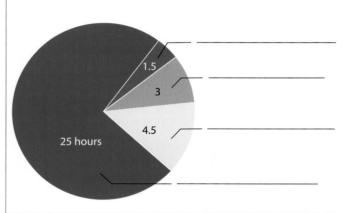

C PERSONALIZE Think of a subject, activity, or skill you are currently learning. Then complete the tasks.

1. Draw a pie chart that shows how much time you spend learning this thing each week using different methods: in a class with a teacher, online with a teacher, alone with a tutor or private instructor, or teaching yourself.
2. Then compare your pie chart with some of your classmates' pie charts.

Critical Thinking | **D BRAINSTORM** Write the benefits of each method of education in the chart.

Advantages of Different Methods of Education	
Taking an in-person class	Studying with a tutor/private instructor
Taking an online course	Teaching yourself

SPEAKING SKILL Relate to What Your Audience Knows

Just as using previous knowledge can help you understand new information, making connections to what your listeners are likely to know can help them understand your main points.

There are several effective ways you can link to your listeners' knowledge:

1. Ask questions.

    What special math words do you know?

2. Compare your points to things your listeners will probably know or have experienced.

    Learning math is like learning another language; math equations are like sentences.

3. Support your points with examples or give definitions of words that may not be familiar.

    A math formula is a fact written with mathematical symbols, like $E = mc^2$.

E Look at the short talk below. Underline the parts that connect to what the audience knows.

Recently I learned how to play pickleball. The rules are simple: You hit a ball over a net and try to win points. That sounds like tennis, doesn't it? In fact, if you know tennis, pickleball will be familiar. The two sports *do* have differences, though. In pickleball, the ball is lighter and the playing area—called the court—is smaller than in tennis. Also, pickleball paddles—the things you use to hit the ball—are smaller than tennis rackets. They're like table tennis paddles. Anyway, for me, pickleball's way more enjoyable than tennis, so I really recommend trying it!

F Tell a partner about the most interesting or unusual skill, activity, or subject you have ever learned. Say how you learned it and help them understand by linking to previous knowledge you think they have.

▼ Pickleball players in Jalisco, Mexico

Review

A **VOCABULARY** Complete each sentence with a phrasal verb from the box. TWO phrasal verbs are extra.

believe in	deal with	get into	major in
check out	end up	look after	

1. Are you going to listen to that talk about what subject to _____?

2. Did you _____ the whole website or just the first page?

3. Do you usually _____ your problems or try to forget them?

4. I doubt we'll _____ finishing more than half the project today.

5. You should _____ cooking. It would save you a lot of money.

B **PRONUNCIATION** Complete the words with the correct letters: *mb*, *bt*, *kn*, or *wr*. Then say the words.

1. cli_____   3. _____ite

2. _____ew   4. dou_____

C **GRAMMAR** Say sentences that include these comparatives and superlatives.

1. is one of the most common
2. are usually hotter
3. is larger than
4. is the largest in the world
5. is the most difficult

D **SPEAKING SKILL** Answer the questions so that children could understand. In your answers, link to knowledge that children you know would probably have.

1. What did Masako Wakamiya do?
2. Who is Mike Gil?

RE-ASSESS What skills or language still need improvement?

Final Tasks

OPTION 1 Discuss sayings about education

A **BRAINSTORM** With a partner, share sayings about education from your country or culture and explain what they mean.

B Work in a group. Choose TWO of the sayings and ideas about education below. Discuss what they mean and why you think education is important. Share your ideas with the class.

- It is better to know some of the questions than all of the answers.
- He who laughs most, learns best.
- A good education is a foundation for a better future.
- Education is a continual process. It's like a bicycle . . . if you don't pedal, you don't go forward.
- If you give someone a fish, you feed them for a day. If you teach someone to fish, you feed them for a lifetime.

C After the discussion, consider these questions:

- How do you feel about your participation?
- Did you use the skills and language from this unit?

▼ Students in a technical leadership program in Nairobi, Kenya

See Unit 6 Rubric in the Appendix.

OPTION 2 Present on something you want to study

A MODEL Listen to someone present on something he wants to study. Complete the notes. 🔊

What does the speaker want to learn?	1_____ (also called Japanese chess)
What does the speaker say about this topic?	It is similar to 2_____ but also different from it.
What reasons does the speaker give for wanting to learn this topic?	• To learn more about his 3_____ • To be better at critical 4_____
How will the speaker know he learned his topic?	• He can understand different 5_____ • He can start to 6_____ at his level

---

PRESENTATION SKILL Check Understanding

When giving a presentation, it's important to check that your listeners understand you. Here are some ways to do this:

1. Look at the faces and body language of people in your audience. You may be able to see whether anyone is confused or not following what you are saying.
2. Stop and ask, "Any questions?" Then wait for a few seconds to allow the audience time to decide if they want to ask you something.
3. Ask questions to confirm that your audience understands. For example, if you are talking about a subject you want to study, you could ask if listeners know what this subject is, ask them how similar it is to other subjects, ask them to name some famous people related to the subject, and so on.

B ANALYZE THE MODEL Listen again and answer each question with a number. 🔊

1. How many times does the speaker check understanding? _____
2. How many reasons does he give for wanting to learn *shogi*? _____

C PLAN Think of something you want to study in the future. It could be a subject you want to major in, a topic you want to learn more about, or even a skill you could use to help others. Make notes about what you will say. Use the chart above as a guide.

D Think about ways you will check that people understand your talk. Add to your plan some notes about questions you can ask or things you can do.

E PRACTICE AND PRESENT Practice giving your presentation to a partner before you present it to the class.

OUR CHANGING WORLD 7

Rock towers at the bottom of Mono Lake in California, USA, formed over many centuries. They are visible now because the water level has fallen due to human activity. Above water, the rock towers are eroded, or worn away by wind and water.

IN THIS UNIT, YOU WILL:

- Watch or listen to a talk about Earth science
- Watch a video on earthquakes
- Listen to a discussion about scientific ideas
- Create a list for a disaster supplies kit
  OR Talk about a change in our world

THINK AND DISCUSS:

1. What are natural ways that the planet changes?
2. What are ways that humans change the planet?
3. What environmental changes have you noticed?

Look at the information. Then answer the questions.

1. What environmental changes do the captions mention?

2. How have humans contributed to these changes?

3. What solutions have humans found to adapt to the changes?

Environmental
ADAPTATION

In Ladakh, India, fresh water that melts from the glaciers in the spring is used for watering crops. Because of global warming, the glaciers now continue to melt during the winter. By controlling the direction of the water to create ice pyramids, called *ice stupas*, people are able to save the water for when they need it.

Holes, called *lavaka* in the Malagasy language, have formed in the hills of central Madagascar because humans have cut down so many trees there. Farmers realized the dirt within the lavakas was especially good for growing food and so adapted to the environmental change.

In Bangladesh, farmland can be under water for half of the year because of seasonal flooding. To adapt, people make floating gardens called *baira* out of bamboo and water hyacinth. The floating gardens allow people to grow food all year long.

A Vocabulary

A **MEANING FROM CONTEXT** Look at the infographic and listen to the information. Notice the words in blue and think about their meanings. 🔊

EARTH'S FOUR SYSTEMS

Earth is our home. It's the **source** of everything we need, from the food we eat to the valuable resources, such as oil and metals, that we need to make and use everyday products. Because it's so important, it's not surprising that many people are interested in studying Earth. And it's a huge topic to study. It's so **broad**, in fact, that the subject is often divided into four aspects called **systems** or spheres. These **cover** the main systems of our planet: the lithosphere, hydrosphere, biosphere, and atmosphere. These names sound **technical**, but in simple terms, they are Earth's rocks, water, life, and air.

These systems seem **separate** from each other, but scientists **emphasize** that they are connected. The hydrosphere and atmosphere, for example, are both **essential** for life. Moreover, **events** that affect one sphere can have an effect on other systems, too. For example, an earthquake can make rocks move and cause large ocean waves. These moving rocks and powerful waves can kill animals and people. Serious natural disasters like this are relatively **rare**, although global warming is causing other kinds to increase.

Lithosphere – rocks

Atmosphere – air

Hydrosphere – water

Biosphere – life

B Complete the definitions with the correct form of the words from exercise A.

1. ~~broad~~ *technical* (adj) hard to understand; related to a specific subject
2. *essential* (adj) necessary
3. *rare* (adj) not common; unusual
4. *separate* (adj) different
5. ~~technical~~ *broad* (adj) including many things
6. *events* (n) a thing that happens or takes place
7. ~~emphasize~~ *system* (n) a group of things that work together
8. *source* (n) where something comes from
9. *cover* (v) to include or deal with something
10. ~~system~~ *emphasize* (v) to show that something is important

C Complete the sentences with the words from exercise B.

1. Although natural disasters aren't common, they aren't *rare* either, and *events* like these can cause a lot of damage, especially when people aren't prepared.
2. American college students can take a ~~system~~ *broad* range of classes in their first two years.
3. Medical students must understand the ~~broad~~ *system* of the body, such as the one used for eating and digestion.
4. Professors often ~~source~~ ~~essential~~ *emphasize* important points and ideas by repeating them or highlighting them.
5. Parts of the speaker's talk were too *technical*; only a few experts could understand her.
6. A good textbook will *cover* important information on a subject.
7. The instructor said it was ~~emphasize~~ *essential* that students do their work on time, or they would fail.
8. The professor told students to submit the three homework assignments as *separate* files.
9. Websites can be a good ~~essential~~ *sources* of information, but don't trust everything you find online.

D Work with a partner. Find the prepositions that can be used after these words from exercise A. Then create a new sentence for each word and preposition.

1. source *of* : *Oranges are a good source of vitamin C.*
2. essential _____ : _____
3. separate _____ : _____

Listening Studying Earth Science

Critical Thinking | **A** **PREDICT** Listen to an excerpt from a talk. Then work in a group. Discuss who the speaker probably is and where the talk probably takes place. 🔊

Earth science

Eliots

LISTENING SKILL **Understand the Purpose of a Talk**

Speakers give talks for various reasons, including to give information, persuade their audience, or entertain. Identifying a speaker's purpose can help you better understand and react to their words. For instance, you might listen more critically if a speaker's goal is to change your mind rather than make you laugh.

In some cases, a speaker will directly state their purpose in the introduction *(My goal today is to . . .)* or in the conclusion *(The purpose of my talk was to . . .)*. In other cases, you may be able to recognize the purpose by asking yourself questions and listening for the answers.

Who is the speaker?   *What ideas do they repeat?*   *Who is the audience?*
What is their main point?   *Where is the talk taking place?*

▼ An entomologist, a scientist who studies insects, at work in Madagascar

B **MAIN IDEAS** Watch or listen and then answer the questions. 🔊 ▶

1. What is the speaker's main purpose?
   a. To contrast Earth science with other subjects
   b. To introduce Earth science to college students ✓
   c. To explain important Earth science theories
   d. To persuade students to major in Earth science

2. What topics does the speaker discuss? Choose TWO answers.
   a. What Earth science is ✓
   b. Why Earth science is hard
   c. How Earth science is special ✓
   d. Who teaches Earth science

3. What points does the speaker make about Earth Science? Choose TWO answers.
   a. It's broad and involves different fields. ✓
   b. It's less popular now than it used to be.
   c. It's mainly about studying natural disasters.
   d. It's a good degree choice in many ways. ✓

C **DETAILS** Listen again. Read the statements. Write T for *True* or F for *False*. 🔊

The speaker . . .

1. __T__ tells students they can ask other questions between 10 and 12 tomorrow.
2. __F__ lists two of Earth's four systems: the biosphere and the hydrosphere. *water rocks, planet,*
3. __T__ says the four different systems, or areas, of Earth science are connected.
4. __F__ mentions that Earth scientists can predict and prevent natural disasters. *we can't prevent*
5. __F__ says finding new sources of essential rare earth elements would be typical.
6. __T__ explains why majoring in Earth science can help students get a job.

D **RECALL** Compare your answers to exercise C with a partner. Then discuss how to correct the false statements so they are true. | Critical Thinking

E **FOCUSED LISTENING** Read the information. Then listen to the excerpts and complete the figurative expressions you hear. Finally, match each expression to its meaning. 🔊

> Figurative language can express an idea indirectly by saying it is like something else. For example, a teacher might say a student's essay is *like a novel* to suggest it is very long.

1. __d__ to get the ball (dropping / *rolling*)   a. to be a way to achieve something
2. __b__ to (*paint* / take) a picture of something   b. to describe something
3. __c__ to open (*doors* / windows)   c. to give special opportunities
4. __a__ to be a (journey / *ticket*) to something   d. to start something

Speaking

A **ANALYZE** In Listening A, the speaker talked about Earth science and some of the skills people who study it can develop. Discuss these questions in a group.

1. Look at the photo and read the caption. What skills do the scientists doing the tornado research need? Are those skills important in other jobs, too?
2. What are important skills that people need these days to have success in life?

SPEAKING SKILL **Use Linking Words**

Linking words show relationships between ideas. We use them in several ways, including to:

Add information: *Furthermore, . . .* *In addition, . . .* *. . . , too*
*Earthquakes can be dangerous. Floods can be deadly, **too**.*

Show contrast: *However, . . .* *On the other hand, . . .* *In contrast, . . .*
*Earthquakes can be dangerous. **However**, serious quakes are rare.*

Give an example: *For example, . . .* *. . . , for instance, . . .* *. . . such as . . .*
*Earthquakes can be dangerous. The 1755 Lisbon quake, **for instance**, killed up to 50,000.*

Scientists in a research vehicle observe a tornado near Dodge City, Kansas, USA. Their mission is to get a device inside the tornado to collect information about it.

B Complete the sentences with linking words from the skill box. The punctuation will help you decide which ones are appropriate. In some cases, more than one answer is possible.

1. Earth science is a popular major. _____, it's not as popular as business or health science.

2. Ontario, Canada, has many beautiful natural places, _____ Niagara Falls and Algonquin Provincial Park.

3. Earthquakes are common in Japan. _____, the country regularly experiences major storms called typhoons.

4. On the one hand, farmers need rain to help crops grow. _____, too much rain can cause dangerous floods.

5. China is one of the largest countries in the world. Brazil and India are both large, _____ .

C On a separate piece of paper, write TWO sentences for each pair of words below. Use linking words from the box to show the relationships between the ideas in the sentences.

1. students and teachers
2. phones and computers
3. vocabulary and grammar

PRONUNCIATION Dropped Consonants

🔊 Consonant clusters can be hard to pronounce. To make them easier to say, we often omit, or leave out, certain consonant sounds. Two common examples are the /d/ sound in words that end with *-nds* and the /t/ sound in words that end with *-cts* or *-nts*:

diamonds /daᵞmənz/	friends /frɛnz/	hands /hænz/	sounds /saʷnz/
effects /əfɛks/	events /əvɛnz/	facts /fæks/	prints /prins/

D Listen to the sentences and cross out the letters *t* and *d* that are omitted. 🔊

1. My parents are history teachers.
2. It's so cold. My hands are freezing!
3. Think about all the facts before you decide.
4. Are your friends coming to dinner?
5. People felt the effects of the flood for years.
6. During the winter, they spend most weekends skiing.
7. One person counts while the other person hides.
8. Hold on! It will only take a few more seconds.
9. Do you follow the latest fashion trends?
10. How many tents do you think we'll need?

E With a partner, practice the sentences in exercise D. When you speak, first say and then omit the /d/ and /t/ sounds you marked. Which way is easier for you to pronounce?

GRAMMAR FOR SPEAKING Time Words and Expressions

We use adverbs or time expressions to talk about the time of an action (when) or the frequency of an action (how often).

When: *(two days/a year) ago, at (night/noon), after/before (class), in (the future), last/next (week/month), now, soon, today, yesterday*

> *A big storm will hit us* **soon***. I'm glad we prepared for it* **yesterday***.*

How often: *always, every (day/week), once/three times (a week/month), never, occasionally, often, rarely, sometimes, usually*

> *I'm* **rarely** *late, but my sister's the opposite. She* **never** *arrives on time!*

Note: adverbs of frequency come after the verb *be* but before other verbs.

F Underline the time words and expressions. Then say the conversation with a partner.

A: Have you decided what major you'll choose in the fall?

B: Well, I did some Earth science projects last semester, and it really interests me. And two of my friends told me yesterday that they're going to major in Earth science. But I don't want to disappoint my dad. He always tells me I should do math.

A: It definitely sounds like you should pick Earth science. And the university lets you take two majors now, so you could also do math.

B: Oh, right! I forgot about that. When did they make that change?

A: I remember hearing about it last year.

B: I rarely pay attention to the college updates, but I guess I should! I'm glad I ran into you today.

G Choose the correct time word or expression to complete each sentence. Compare answers with a partner. Discuss why the incorrect expression is wrong.

1. A big earthquake happened (next week / two days ago); luckily, nobody was hurt.

2. Earth science is becoming more and more popular with students (every / last) year.

3. If you get up early, you will (usually / rarely) be late for class or other appointments.

4. The professor told her students that she would give them a test (recently / soon).

5. The student found a job just (twice a week / two weeks) after she finished college.

6. Why don't you ever reply to your messages? I've texted you (many times / once)!

H **PERSONALIZE** Choose a time word or expression to complete each question. Then interview a partner.

1. What is one item you are planning to buy (later today / soon / next week)?

2. How many movies did you watch (recently / last week / last month)?

3. What is one subject you might like to study (next year / in the future)?

4. What is one thing you must do (today / tomorrow / soon) but don't want to?

5. Where is one place you have got to go (later today / in a few days)?

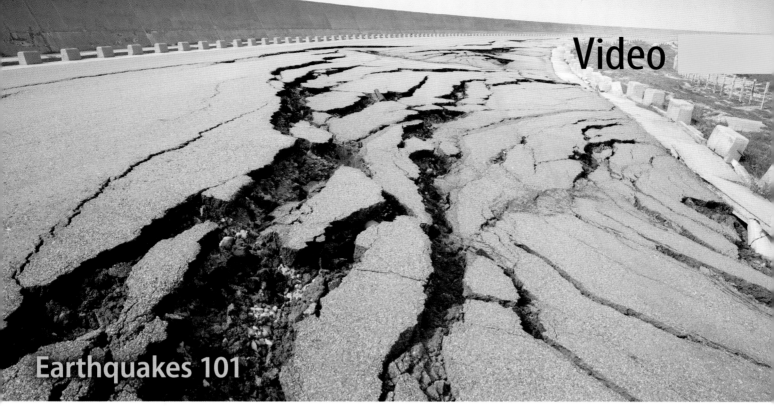

Video

Earthquakes 101

pressure (n) the physical force put on an object
emit (v) to send out
drill (n) repeated practice of what to do in an emergency

devastation (n) serious damage caused by an event
feature (n) a distinctive part of something

▲ A cracked road in Haiti after an earthquake

A Watch the video. Check the ideas that are covered. ▶

1. _____ How often very big earthquakes happen

2. _____ How to protect communities from quakes

3. _____ The three main causes of earthquakes

4. _____ Where earthquakes happen in the world

B Watch again. Choose the correct words to complete the sentences. ▶

1. About 80 percent of earthquakes occur at the (circum-Pacific belt / mid-Atlantic ridge).
2. Earthquakes are mainly caused by (volcanoes / movement of tectonic plates).
3. Tectonic plates move against each other in (just one or two / up to four) different ways.
4. Ideas to protect communities from quakes include (building bridges / educating people).

C **PERSONALIZE** At the end of the video, the speaker says earthquakes cause damage but can also create "magnificent features" that make our planet a special place to live. What are some beautiful or amazing natural places in your country or in another country? How do they make our world special? Share your ideas with a group.

B Vocabulary

A Listen and repeat. Check the words you know. 🔊

accept (v)	form (v)	majority (n)	revolution (n)	support (v)
evidence (n)	key (adj)	occur (v)	standard (adj)	surface (n)

B **MEANING FROM CONTEXT** Work with a partner. Discuss which words from exercise A could complete each sentence. Then listen and write the words you hear. 🔊

THE BILLION-YEAR THEORY

An important theory in Earth science is that the present is ¹ _____key_____ to understanding the past. For example, we can see valleys ² _____form_____ and get deeper when water flows across the ³ _____surface_____ of low areas of land between hills or mountains. From this, we can infer that a valley with no river today did have water that passed through it at some point. In other words, we can generally understand the events and processes of the past if we study what ⁴ _____occurs_____ today.

These days, all Earth scientists ⁵ _____accept_____ this idea. But when James Hutton first suggested the theory in 1785, no one, except for a few people, believed it. Why did the ⁶ _____majority_____ of experts not accept it? Because if Hutton was right, it would suggest two things. First, that Earth was very old. And second, that tiny actions repeated over a long time could have an effect on the planet. At the time, however, the ⁷ _____standard_____ thinking was that Earth was young and that only huge, sudden events, such as earthquakes, could affect it.

But Hutton felt he was right. He and the others who believed him began to look for examples to ⁸ _____support_____ his theory. They soon found them in the rocks of Scotland, Hutton's home. As more ⁹ _____evidence_____ was found, it became clear Hutton was right. The present *was* key to the past, and Earth *was* very old. Billions of years old, in fact. This knowledge started a ¹⁰ _____revolution_____ in scientific thinking that led to many other important ideas.

▼ A valley in Al Bahah, Saudi Arabia

C Complete the sentences with the correct form of the words from exercise A.

1. ___evidence___ is information that shows that something is true.

2. A ___revolution___ is an important change in how people think or act.

3. If something ___occurs___, it happens, often without planning.

4. If something is ___key___, it is extremely important.

5. If something is ___standard___, people think it is usual and correct.

6. Information that ___support___ a theory is information that shows it is true.

7. The ___majority___ of a group is the larger part of that group.

8. The ___surface___ of something is the outside or top part of it.

9. To ___accept___ a theory or an opinion means to believe that it is correct.

10. To ___form___ something means to create it or cause it to exist.

VOCABULARY SKILL   Commonly Confused Words

Some pairs of words are easily confused because the two words look similar, sound similar, or have similar meanings. For example:

*Sunshine can **affect** how people feel. Many people report a positive **effect**.*

*I'm afraid that I don't **accept** anything the speaker said **except** his last point.*

*I **passed** by my old high school yesterday. I can't believe my teenage years are in the **past**.*

To avoid mistakes, carefully study what easily confused words mean and how they are used.

D The box gives SIX examples of easily confused words. Find and underline these six words in exercise B. Then complete the definitions.

1. _____ (conj/prep) not including

2. _____ (n) the result of something

3. ___accept___ (v) to believe or agree with an idea

4. _____ (v) to change or influence

5. _____ (v) to have gone by something or someone

6. _____ (n) the time before the present

E **IDENTIFY** Work in a group. Write the second word in each commonly confused pair. Then discuss how the two words in each pair are different. Use a dictionary if necessary.

Critical Thinking

1. advise / ___advice___

2. desert / _____

3. its / _____

4. lose / _____

5. their / _____

6. to / _____

Listening   A Revolution in Earth Science

Critical Thinking | **A**   **RECOGNIZE**   Work in a group. Look at the map of Earth from about 335 million years ago. Label the modern continents and subcontinent and discuss how each one has moved since it was part of Pangaea.

> Africa   Australia   Antarctica   Europe and Asia   ~~India~~   North America   South America

1 *North America*

2 *South America*

3 *Antarctica*

4 *Europe and Asia* ~~*Asia*~~

5 *Africa*

6 India

7 *Australia*

▲ The supercontinent "Pangaea" that Alfred Wegener suggested in 1920

B   **MAIN IDEAS**   Listen to a class discussion and take notes. Then choose the correct words to complete the sentences. 🔊

1. The students in this class are probably studying (Earth science / science history).
2. The main purpose of this lecture is to explain (paradigm shifts / plate tectonics).
3. The main focus of the discussion is on the (reaction to / source of) Wegener's idea.

NOTE-TAKING SKILL   Take Note of Steps in a Process

Processes often have stages, or steps. Making a note of these can help you understand the process better. To recognize stages, listen for:

- Sequence words and time expressions, such as *first, second, before this, after that, last,* and *finally*. These make the order of the stages clear.

- The order in which the speaker describes the stages. This is usually the order in which the steps happen.

Use numbers or bullets to list steps.

1. *Wegener noticed that some continents looked like they would fit together.*
2. *He looked for evidence to support this idea.*
3. *He found evidence.*
4. *He developed a theory that the continents moved over time.*

C Listen to an excerpt. Number the stages of a paradigm shift in the order they occur. 🔊

a. _1_ Somebody suggests a new theory.

b. _3_ People find supporting evidence.

c. _4_ More people believe the new idea.

d. _5_ The new theory becomes the standard.

e. _2_ Most people don't accept the new idea.

D **DETAILS** Listen to the discussion again and add to your notes. Complete each statement with a phrase from the box. TWO phrases are extra. 🔊

false information	human activity	new evidence	puzzle pieces
germ theory	important changes	popular ideas	rock plates

1. Earth's surface is formed of ___rock plates___ that move slowly over many years.

2. Wegener noticed some continents looked like ___Puzzle Pieces___ that fit together.

3. Paradigm shifts are ___important changes___ in the standard way that people think.

4. Usually, paradigm shifts occur over a long time as ___new evidence___ is found.

5. The ___germ theory___ of how disease occurs is a good example of a paradigm shift.

6. These days, many people think CO_2 from ___human activity___ affects Earth's climate.

E Share your notes with a partner and complete the chart by checking the correct columns to match the theories to their academic subjects.

	Astronomy	Earth Science	Medical Science
Germs cause diseases			✓
Human activity affects the climate		✓	
Planets go around the sun	✓		
Plate tectonics		✓	

F **FOCUSED LISTENING** Complete the sentence with the easily confused words you hear. When do we use each word? 🔊

And [1]_____ over time, people found more evidence, and so, more and more

people accepted the idea [2]_____ didn't accept it.

B Speaking

Critical Thinking | **A** **EVALUATE** In Listening B, the speakers discussed paradigm shifts in scientific thinking. We can also think of paradigm shifts in how people act in society. Discuss how the COVID-19 pandemic caused a paradigm shift in how people think and act in these areas: education, health, travel, and work.

CRITICAL THINKING   Make Inferences

To make inferences, or infer, means to understand something that is suggested rather than stated directly. For example, if a friend says, "I almost fell asleep when I went to a movie yesterday," you can infer that your friend was tired and/or that the movie was boring.

It's common for information to be expressed indirectly in speech, writing, or even images. As a result, being able to make inferences is an important skill.

Critical Thinking | **B** Work with a partner. Practice saying the conversation. Then discuss what you can infer about the things below.

LEE: Hi, Sam. Are you going to a class?

SAM: Actually, I just had one. I'm going to the library to study.

LEE: You OK? You look pretty upset about something.

SAM: I just learned my score on a test I took last week.

LEE: I guess you didn't . . . Oh, wow! Did you just feel the ground move?

SAM: Yeah! Luckily, that was just a small one. Let's hope we don't get a big one!

1. What the people do
2. Sam's test score
3. What just happened

Critical Thinking | **C** **INFER** Read the paragraph about a lake. With a partner, decide which of the statements can most reasonably be inferred. Choose Yes or No.

It's easy to see the bottom of the lake and the many fish that are swimming around. A path goes all the way around the lake. The path is flat and wide. Several people are walking along the path; some are walking dogs. No one is swimming.

1. The water is clear.	Yes	No
2. The lake is a good place for walking.	Yes	No
3. It's a beautiful day.	Yes	No
4. Dogs are allowed at the lake.	Yes	No
5. It's too cold for swimming.	Yes	No

D **INFER** With a partner, discuss what inferences you can make about each situation. Critical Thinking

1. Yasmin is yawning. She had a paper due this morning.
2. John has started going to the gym every day.
3. The price of oranges has gone up recently.
4. There's less traffic in the city this week.

E **INFER** Look at the photo and read the caption. With a group, discuss some inferences you can make. Critical Thinking

A: Look at the huge ash cloud! We can definitely infer that it's dangerous.
B: Really? For me, it doesn't look dangerous because the people are still playing golf.

▼ People play golf as an ash cloud rises in the distance from the Kilauea volcano on Hawaii's "Big Island."

Review

SELF-ASSESS

How well can you . . . ?	Very well.	OK.	I need improvement.
use the key vocabulary	☐	☐	☐
recognize dropped consonants	☐	☐	☐
use linking words	☐	☐	☐
use time words and expressions	☐	☐	☐

A VOCABULARY Complete the pairs of synonyms and antonyms with words from the box.

believe	happen	minority	simple	usual
destroy	include	narrow	together	vital

Synonyms

1. ______________ / accept
2. ______________ / cover
3. ______________ / essential
4. ______________ / occur
5. ______________ / standard

Antonyms

6. ______________ / broad
7. ______________ / form
8. ______________ / majority
9. ______________ / separate
10. ______________ / technical

B PRONUNCIATION Check the words in which the underlined *t* or *d* can be omitted. Then say the words.

1. ____ aspec<u>t</u>s
2. ____ plane<u>t</u>s
3. ____ suppor<u>t</u>s
4. ____ thousan<u>d</u>s
5. ____ continen<u>t</u>s
6. ____ lea<u>d</u>s

C GRAMMAR AND SPEAKING SKILL Underline the time words and expressions. Then complete the sentences using a linking word to add information, show a contrast, or give an example.

1. I have a big test tomorrow . . .
2. My family usually eats dinner together . . .
3. Earth science will always be necessary . . .
4. I will be on vacation next week . . .
5. The earth always amazes me . . .

RE-ASSESS **What skills or language need improvement?**

Final Tasks

OPTION 1 Create a list for a disaster supplies kit

A Work in a group. Discuss the following questions.

1. Look at the photo. What does "Tsunami Hazard Zone" mean?
2. Why is the sign near the shore?
3. What kinds of damage can a tsunami cause to cities and communities?
4. What kinds of damage can other natural disasters cause to cities and communities?

B BRAINSTORM With a partner, brainstorm a list of things to include in a disaster supplies kit, which is a collection of basic things you would need in case of an emergency. Consider these questions as you make your list:

- What will you eat and drink?
- What will you wear?
- What tools will you need?
- How much money will you need?
- What important documents will you need?
- What other special needs do you have? (e.g., medications, pet food, etc.)

C DISCUSS Form a group with another pair of students. Share your ideas for your disaster supplies kits.

Monterey, California, USA

OPTION 2 Talk about a change in our world

A **MODEL** Listen to two students give a joint presentation on a change in our world. Complete the notes with ONE word or a number that the speakers say. 🔊

What is the topic?	Topic: Plastic in the [1]_____
What does the first speaker say?	Plastic invented about [2]_____ years ago Only about [3]_____ percent of plastic is recycled Tiny plastic pieces get into the [4]_____ we eat
What does the second speaker say?	People are changing their [5]_____ : → using less plastic and recycling more [6]_____ have found bacteria that eat plastic

COLLABORATION SKILL Give a Joint Presentation

Giving an effective joint presentation requires communication with your partner(s) and with the audience. Before you give your presentation, discuss who will say each point. Practice your presentation and give each other feedback on how to improve. At the beginning of your presentation, you can introduce yourselves and explain who will say what. If you repeat a key point, remind the audience it was said before by saying, "As my partner mentioned, . . ."

🔊 **ONLINE** If you are presenting online, have one person control the presentation. When you are finished your turn, say, "Now my partner will talk about . . ."

B **ANALYZE THE MODEL** Listen again. Check the statements that are true. 🔊

1. _____ The speakers suggest that few things are made of plastic these days.

2. _____ The speakers suggest that people caused the problem of plastic pollution.

3. _____ One speaker repeated a key point and reminded the audience who said it first.

4. _____ You can infer that the speakers feel the situation will improve in the future.

C **PLAN** Work with a partner. Complete the steps.

1. Choose an environmental change you will talk about and consider how it has impacted people. This could be a sudden change caused by a natural disaster, a natural change that occurred over a long time, or a change caused by human activity.

2. Do some research if you wish and make notes about what you will say about the change. Describe some ways your community or others are responding to the change.

3. Organize your notes and discuss how you will deliver an effective joint presentation.

D **PRACTICE AND PRESENT** Practice giving your presentation with your partner before you present it to the class.

LIVING HISTORY 8

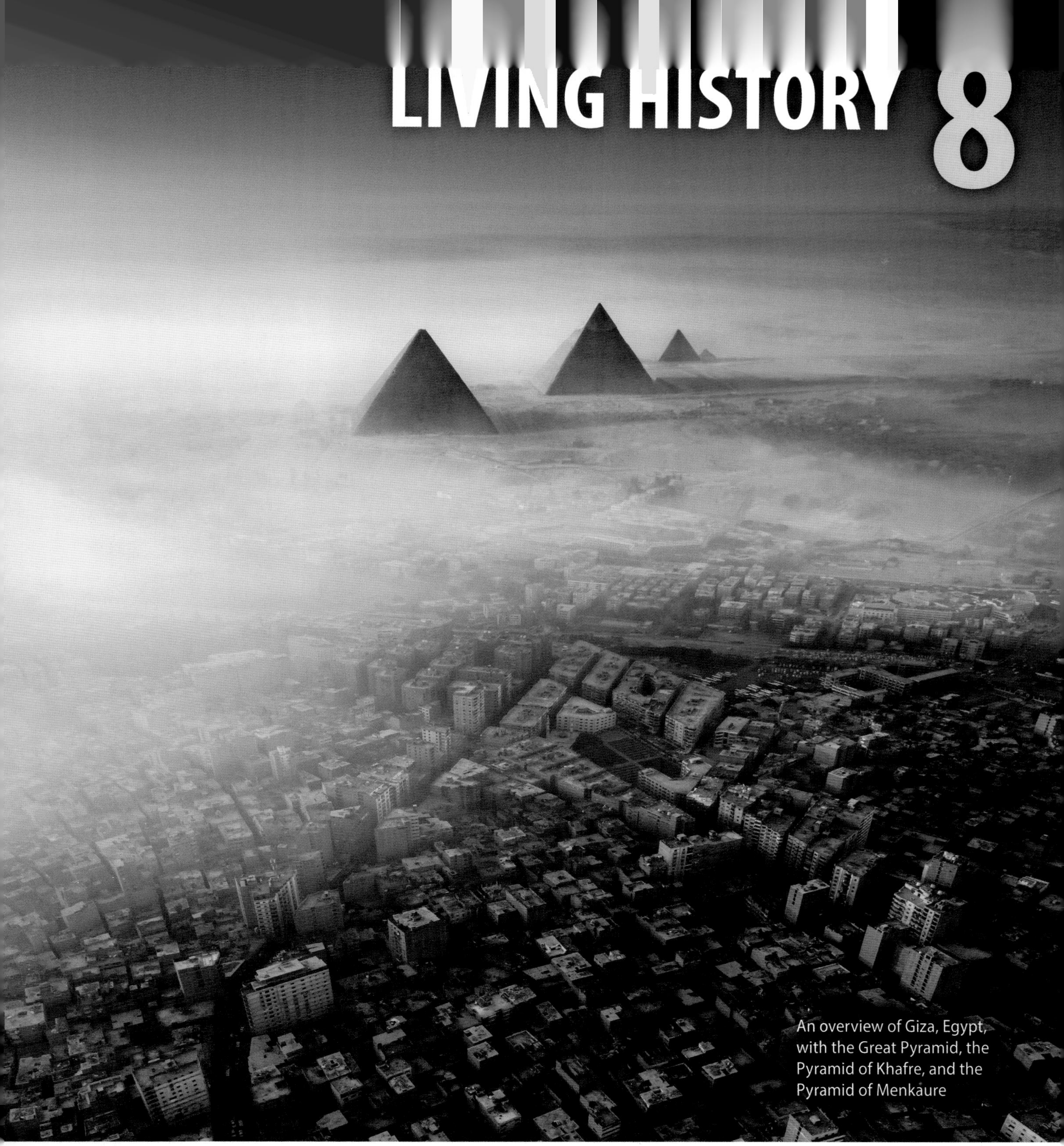

An overview of Giza, Egypt, with the Great Pyramid, the Pyramid of Khafre, and the Pyramid of Menkaure

IN THIS UNIT, YOU WILL:

- Watch or listen to a talk about living museums
- Watch a video on the Rosetta Stone
- Listen to a podcast about community science projects
- Discuss special objects from your past
  OR Present a historical object, site, or person

THINK AND DISCUSS:

1. What do you know about the history of Egypt?

2. Can visiting old buildings, such as the pyramids at Giza, help people understand life in the past?

3. Some people say you have to understand the past to understand the present. Do you agree?

141

Look at the information. Then answer the questions.

1. How is the way Twitty prepares food similar to the way most people cook now? How is it different?

2. How are your food habits similar to your parents' food habits? How are they different?

3. What are some foods you enjoy now that people have been enjoying for a long time? What do you know about the history of these foods?

Interpreting the Past

Have you ever wondered what people in the past ate? Culinary historians study the past by looking at what people ate and drank and how they prepared meals. Understanding the history of food helps them understand culture at different times as well as the effects on what we eat now.

Michael Twitty is an award-winning culinary historian, food writer, and National Geographic Explorer. He works to educate people on the food traditions of African Americans, connecting the past to the present through food.

Michael Twitty and Stefanie Dunn, a domestic arts specialist, prepare a meal at Colonial Williamsburg, an open-air museum in the USA, using traditional methods and ingredients.

A Vocabulary

A Listen and repeat. Check the words you know. 🔊

alive (adj)	**authentic** (adj)	**experience** (v)	**interpret** (v)	**purpose** (n)
ancient (adj)	**demonstration** (n)	**institution** (n)	**preserve** (v)	**site** (n)

B **MEANING FROM CONTEXT** Read and listen to the information. Notice the words in blue and think about their meanings. 🔊

THE HISTORY OF MUSEUMS

Ancient Museums
There were museums in **ancient** times, but they were more similar to modern colleges than modern museums. They displayed books, art, and other important objects, but these **institutions** were mainly places for people to learn about and discuss ideas.

Early Museums
Then in the 1700s in Europe, studying the past became fashionable. People started visiting ancient **sites** to find, buy, or sometimes just take wonders from the past—historical objects that are especially beautiful or important. They would then display these objects in "wonder rooms" in their homes. These private museums were not open to everyone; only the wealthy were able to visit.

Early Modern Museums
Over time, the **purpose** of these early museums changed. They opened to the public and focused more on educating people. Museums also realized they needed to **preserve** the objects. They developed ways to protect them and keep them safe for everyone to see. They also hired experts to **interpret** the objects so visitors could understand them better.

Modern Museums
These days, some museums take different forms. For example, outdoor living museums let visitors **experience** life in the past. They preserve **authentic** historical buildings, and their interpreters keep the past **alive** by giving **demonstrations** of how people did things long ago.

Future Museums
What changes and developments will we see next in museums? For instance, will some museums decide to return important historical objects to their original countries and put copies of these wonders on display instead, and will online museums become more popular than traditional ones?

C Complete each definition with the correct word from exercise A.

1. A(n) _demonstration_ (n) involves showing someone how to do something.
2. A(n) _purpose_ (n) is a reason for something.
3. A(n) _ancient_ (adj) thing is from a long time ago or is very old.
4. A(n) _site_ (n) is a place where something was built or happened.
5. A(n) _institution_ (n) is a large, important organization.
6. If you _interpret_ (v) something, you explain it to other people.
7. Something _authentic_ (adj) is real or true.
8. To _experience_ (v) something is to feel it or have it happen to you.
9. When something is _alive_ (adj), it is living, not dead.
10. When you _preserve_ (v) something, you keep it in good condition.

VOCABULARY SKILL   Negative Prefixes and Suffixes

For some words, adding a prefix can give it a negative or opposite meaning. Common negative prefixes include:

dis-	**dis**advantage	**in-**	**in**effective	**non-**	**non**standard
im-	**im**possible	**mis-**	**mis**understand	**un-**	**un**familiar

For some words, the suffix *-less* gives the word a negative meaning. The opposite of *-less* is *-ful*.

end	end**less**	power	power**less** (power**ful**)

D Make words with the opposite meanings using prefixes or suffixes from the skill box. You will use one prefix TWO times. Use a dictionary if needed.

1. able _unable / disable_
2. authentic _inauthentic_
3. important _unimportant_
4. similar _dissimilar_
5. behave _misbehave_
6. useful _useless_

E Work in a group. The paragraph on future museums in "The History of Museums" in exercise B asks "What changes and developments will we see next in museums?" Discuss how you would answer this question.

Listening Preserving the Past

Critical Thinking | **A** **ACTIVATE** Work with a partner. Look at the photo and read the caption. Then discuss what you could learn from entering the farmhouse or speaking to the woman.

B **MAIN IDEAS** Watch or Listen. Which FIVE points does the speaker mainly discuss? 🔊 ▶

a. ___✗___ How good living museums are at preserving the past

b. ___✗___ How living museums are different from other museums

c. ___✗___ How interpreters who work at living museums act

d. ___✗___ What living museums are and what these institutions do

e. ___✗___ What interpreters who work at living museums do

f. ___✗___ What things visitors to living museums can see and do

g. _____ Why living museums have become so popular recently

NOTE-TAKING SKILL   Use Charts

Using a chart can be an effective way to organize your notes when a speaker discusses different aspects of a topic or point. Dividing the information into rows and columns can help you recognize or show the relationship between these different parts.

C **DETAILS** Listen again. Complete the notes with ONE word that the speaker says. 🔊

Living museums like Minseok Folk Village involve all five senses of visitors:

Sight	• ¹ ~~Preserve~~ _building_ from the past and people wearing clothes from the past, too • people use original methods/tools to make things: e.g., traditional ² ~~stuff~~ _medicines_ or pots for *kimchi*
Sound	• accents and music of the time • perhaps also sounds of ³ _horses_ in street
Touch	• traditional clothes and ⁴ _objects_
Smell	• wood used to build some tools and houses
Taste	• traditional dishes from ⁵ ~~onsite~~ the _restaurant_ on site

Two kinds of interpreters work at living museums:

First-person	• wear historical clothes and give ⁶ ~~examples~~ _demonstration_ • talk to visitors like people from past but only about ⁷ _people_ ~~people~~ from past _topics_
Third-person	• same as first-person but speak from modern point of view

A woman wearing traditional clothes works outside a farmhouse from 1850 at an outdoor museum in Lejre, Denmark. The woman is an interpreter whose job is to tell visitors about what life was like in that period.

experience

wonder of history – الاكتشاف

LISTENING SKILL   Recognize Examples

Speakers may give examples to support or explain an idea or to define a word. Recognizing examples will help you understand the speaker's idea or point.

*Museums often display important artifacts from the past, **such as jewelry or pots**.*

Listen for phrases that introduce examples. These phrases often come before the example.

For example, / For instance, . . .   *A good example / illustration (is) . . .*
Take . . . , for example.   *. . . such as / like / including . . .*
. . . , say . . . , for instance.   *. . . (is) a good example / illustration.*

D Match the examples to the speaker's points. 🔊

1. __a__ wonders of history   a. death mask of Pakal

2. __d__ living museums   b. interpreters at Colonial Williamsburg

3. __c__ things made with authentic   c. traditional medicines and large pots for
        methods and tools   storing *kimchi*

4. __b__ first-person interpreters   d. Minseok Village

E **FOCUSED LISTENING** Listen to an excerpt and check the things that are true. 🔊

☑ Living museums are imperfect.   ☑ Interpreters can misunderstand the past.
☑ Experts help living museums be authentic.   ☐ Living museums are time machines.

F **EVALUATE** Do you think people mainly go to living history museums to learn about the past or to have fun? | Critical Thinking

A Speaking

GRAMMAR FOR SPEAKING   Infinitives of Purpose

Infinitives of purpose answer the question *Why?* We use them to express the purpose of, or reason for, an action.

*In ancient times, people visited museums **to discuss** ideas.*

To express a reason for not doing something, add *not* before *to*.

*In ancient times, people visited museums to discuss ideas, **not to see** objects on display.*

We sometimes use *in order* before the infinitive, especially in formal situations, to make it clear that we are expressing the purpose of the action.

*In the 1700s, people began to visit ancient sites **in order to find** objects from the past.*

A Read this summary of the history of museums. Underline the infinitives of purpose.

Museums have a long history. Over time, their purpose has changed. At first, people visited them to discuss ideas. Later, people went to see important objects there. These days, museums want to educate visitors. In order to do this, they hire experts to explain things. Some museums are also thinking about their collections in order to decide whether or not to return some especially important objects to the places they are from.

B Rewrite these sentences using infinitives of purpose. Compare answers with a partner.

1. The experts visited the site. They wanted to look for important or valuable objects.

   The experts visited the site to look for important or valuable object

2. The woman went to the library because she needed to research the Rosetta Stone.

   The woman went to the library to research the Rosetta stone

3. The family bought museum tickets. They were interested in seeing the special exhibition.

   The family bought museum tickets to see the special exhibition

4. The student hoped to learn more about ancient Egypt, so he watched a documentary.

   The student watched a documentary to learn about ancient Egypt

5. The woman read some history books because she wanted to know more about the past.

   The woman read some history books to know more about the past

6. We preserve historical objects. We want to be sure future generations can appreciate them.

   We preserve historical objects to be sure future generation can appreciate them

C **PERSONALIZE** Interview a partner. Use infinitives of purpose in your answers.

1. Where was the last place you visited? Why did you go there?
2. How much was the last thing you bought? Why did you buy it?
3. When was the last time you used your phone? Why did you use it?
4. Who was the last person you contacted? Why did you contact them?

PRONUNCIATION Sentence Stress

🔊 Speakers stress the most important words in a sentence. These are usually content words, which are words that express meaning, such as nouns, verbs, adjectives, and adverbs. In general, the final content word in a sentence is stressed slightly more than the others.

*Museums have a long **history**. Over time, their purpose has **changed**.*

In contrast, speakers usually don't stress function words, such as articles, prepositions, conjunctions, or helping verbs, which show grammatical relationships.

D Work with a partner. Underline the content word in each sentence that you think should be stressed the most. Then take turns reading the text aloud.

Uxmal, Mexico, was an ancient Maya city. There are several pyramids there. One of them is called the "Pyramid of the Magician." It is the tallest pyramid at Uxmal. It took about 300 years to build. The pyramid started out small. Over the years, workers added to it several times. In total, archaeologists have found five different structures at the site.

The Pyramid of the Magician in Uxmal, Mexico

CRITICAL THINKING Compare and Contrast

Comparing and contrasting means looking at the similarities and differences among ideas. Some similarities and differences are obvious, while others are harder to recognize without thinking critically about them. Noting similarities and differences helps you to generalize, categorize, sort, and evaluate information. It is a useful skill in many areas of life.

Critical Thinking | **E** Add the letters of the statements to the correct place in the chart.

Traditional museums	Both	Living museums
~~a~~ e	b ~~e~~ f	a d c

a. Their interpreters may act as if they have no knowledge of modern things.
b. They aim to help visitors understand and learn about things from the past.
c. They are usually open-air spaces that visitors walk around.
d. They allow visitors to try on clothes and touch objects.
e. They are usually indoor spaces that display important or valuable historical objects.
f. Their purpose is to preserve authentic things from the past.

F With a group, discuss other aspects of traditional and living museums. Add these to the appropriate places in the Venn diagram.

G Think about your culture (or another culture that you know well) now and in the past. Make notes of differences and similarities in the chart. Then share your ideas with a partner. What did this activity help you understand about your culture?

Past	Both	Present
they was living in a tent, house of clay using a compass	my kids Saudi coffee cooking a traditional food	using a smart phone using google maps

Secrets of Ancient Egypt

carve (v) to cut shapes or words into a hard material like stone

decipher (v) to discover the meaning of unfamiliar writing

▲ The Rosetta Stone

A   Watch the video. Which summary is better? ▶

    a.   Objects in museums can teach us a lot. The Rosetta Stone, which is an important part of Egyptian history, is a good example. The words carved on this stone helped us decipher hieroglyphics and understand ancient Egyptian civilization better.

    b.   Objects like the Rosetta Stone are important for museums. They help bring more visitors to the museums, which allows the museums to buy more ancient objects to display. The visitors can touch the objects and imagine what it was like to live in past times.

B   Watch again. Choose the correct answers. ▶

    1.   The Rosetta Stone is displayed in a museum in (Egypt / France / Great Britain).

    2.   The Rosetta Stone has the same text in (two / three / four) writing systems.

    3.   People first saw hieroglyphics in Egyptian (museums / pyramids / temples).

    4.   Hieroglyphics represent (Egyptian words / Greek words / pictures or symbols).

    5.   There are questions about who the Rosetta Stone (belongs to / is important to / was created by).

C   The Rosetta Stone is an important part of Egyptian cultural history. In a group, discuss some objects that are important parts of the cultural history of your country or another place you know well. Describe the objects and say why they are important.

Vocabulary

A Listen and repeat. Check the words you know. 🔊

analyze (v)	**imagine** (v)	**organize** (v)	**sign up (for)** (v phr)	**the public** (n)
civilization (n)	**method** (n)	**project** (n)	**take part (in)** (v phr)	**volunteer** (v)

B **MEANING FROM CONTEXT** Consider which words from exercise A could complete the sentences. Then listen and write the words you hear. 🔊

CITIZEN SCIENCE

When you think of doing science, what do you ¹ _imagine_ ? You probably think of scientists working in labs, but this is not true for all science ² _projects_ . There are some that allow nonscientists to do important research work.

Scientists sometimes ³ _organize_ and run experiments in which anyone can ⁴ _take part_ . These are called citizen science or community science projects because members of ⁵ _the public_ can work on them. Over the years, such projects have given scientists a lot of useful knowledge.

Perhaps the oldest citizen science project is from Japan. For 1200 years, people in Kyoto have been able to ⁶ _volunteer_ to note the dates when cherry trees look the most beautiful. This information may not seem important, but it helps scientists ⁷ _analyze_ and understand how our climate has changed.

Another project, called "Ancient Lives," gave the general public a chance to help experts understand the ⁸ _civilization_ of ancient Greece and Egypt. Interested people first had to ⁹ _sign up_ online and do some training. After that, they looked at damaged pieces of old documents and typed in the words they saw. Some documents were poems or letters; others described shopping trips from long ago.

Not all citizen science projects are started by scientists. Terry Herbert, a member of the general public, searched for treasure in a field in England in 2009. He found so many gold and silver coins that he had to ask archaeologists for help. They then studied the site using scientific ¹⁰ _methods_ .

C Choose the correct way to complete each definition.

1. A civilization is a well-developed ((country or society) / organization).
2. A method is a way to ((do) / speak about) something.
3. A project is work that (is done quickly / (takes time to do)).
4. The public means all (experts in a topic / (regular people)).
5. To analyze means to study and (teach / (understand)) something.
6. To imagine something means to ((see it in your mind) / talk about it a lot).
7. To organize something is to (begin or end / plan or arrange) it.
8. To sign up for something is to (agree to do / write about) it.
9. To take part in an activity is to do it (on your own / with other people).
10. To volunteer means to do something without (being paid / working hard).

D Complete each definition with a verb or verb phrase from exercise A.

1. Analysts ~~understand~~ *analyze* _____ information or data.
2. Organizers ~~take time to~~ *organize* _____ a project or event.
3. Participants ~~being paid~~ *take part* _____ in an activity. *(work)*
4. Volunteers ~~plan or arrange~~ *volunteer* _____ to do something.

E **PERSONALIZE** Work in a group. Discuss these questions, giving reasons for your answers.

1. Do you think you are better at **analyzing** information or **imagining** things?
2. Have you ever **signed up** and **volunteered** to do something?
3. In general, do you prefer to work alone or to **take part in** group **projects**?
4. What are some common ways that **the public** can learn about past **civilizations**?

Terry Herbert with some of
the treasures he found

Listening Crowd Science

Critical Thinking | **A** **PREDICT** Listen to an excerpt from the podcast you will hear. Which kind of note-taking chart would be the best one to use? 🔊

   a. A chart with two parts: one part for projects you can take part in and one part for projects the speaker likes

   (b) A chart with three parts: one part each for the different community science projects that the speaker is going to discuss

B **MAIN IDEAS** Listen and take notes. Then decide which summary is better. 🔊

   a. The speaker compares the pros and cons of several citizen science projects that involve archaeology: looking for dinosaur bones in Canada, doing online courses to understand old documents, and looking for objects from past European civilizations. The speaker says projects like these are always useful, but some are more useful than others.

   (b) The speaker discusses several ways the public can become involved in archaeology: taking a "dinosaur dig" vacation, signing up for organized online projects, and just reporting ancient objects when you find them. The speaker says these things can help scientists learn new information and can help all of us understand our world better.

C **DETAILS** Listen again. Choose the TWO correct answers to each question. 🔊

   1. As part of her "dinosaur dig" vacation, the speaker

      (a.) found part of a dinosaur that she was allowed to keep.
      (b.) learned the proper scientific way to dig for dinosaurs.
      c. spent three weeks working outside in cold winter weather.
      d. visited museums in Canada to learn more about dinosaurs.

   2. The speaker says that MicroPasts

      (a.) has projects that involve looking at old records and notes.
      (b.) offers various archaeology projects people can do online.
      c. only has projects related to the civilization of ancient Rome.
      (d.) requires volunteers to pay to sign up for online projects.

   3. According to the speaker, the place called "Doggerland"

      (a.) disappeared 9000 years ago partly due to climate change.
      (b.) had a larger population than any other European country.
      c. used to be in the sea to the north of Britain and Europe.
      (d.) was discovered after members of the public found objects.

   4. The speaker believes that

      a. it is impossible for us to imagine what life was like for ancient people.
      b. most people want to learn and to use new knowledge for a purpose.
      c. scientists learn very little from the majority of citizen science projects.
      (d.) we can contribute to science from the comfort of our own homes.

D Listen to the excerpts. Match each example to the excerpt in which you hear it. TWO examples are extra. 🔊

1. ___ a. a project that scientists did not originally organize

2. ___ b. an institution that ran a project on the MicroPasts site

3. ___ c. important information found in old research notes

4. ___ d. objects that members of the public found on beaches

e. organizations that offer community science vacations

f. past civilizations from different places around the world

E **FOCUSED LISTENING** Listen and write the words you hear. Then consider how this is an example of applying and analyzing information. 🔊

We can ¹_____ knowledge and ²_____ such as understanding climate change or recognizing that life in ancient civilizations was familiar in many ways.

F **PERSONALIZE** Discuss the questions with a small group.

1. How interested are you in learning about the past?
2. How can learning about the past help people?

▼ A young girl examines a fossil she has just discovered during a fossil-hunting trip on the "Jurassic Coast" in England.

B Speaking *Cheap*

Critical Thinking | **A** **RECALL** In Vocabulary B and Listening B, you learned about different kinds of community science projects. Which of these options interest you, and why?

a. going on a dinosaur dig vacation
b. learning more about Doggerland
c. noting information about cherry trees
d. searching for lost treasure in a field
e. taking part in a MicroPasts project

had not
hadn't

SPEAKING SKILL   Summarize

Summarizing means to explain in your own words the key points about something you have heard or read. When you give a summary, do not include your opinion about the topic. Instead, include only the most important information that another person would need in order to be able to answer questions about the topic such as *Who, What, When, Where, How,* and *Why?* Be sure to organize the information in a logical way.

B Put the statements about dinosaur dig vacations in the order in which you would include the statements in a summary of these vacations. TWO statements are extra.

1 6

a. ~~2~~ ² "Dinosaur dig" vacations let the public look for fossils. الحفريات

b. ~~X~~ Dinosaurs lived millions of years ago but are dead now.

c. _3_ Experts give nonscientists training before they dig.

d. _5_ Some organizations let people keep what they find.

e. _____ The Canadian province of British Columbia is beautiful.

f. _1_ Various kinds of organizations offer these vacations.

g. _4_ Volunteers and experts both work on the same sites.

Paintings

C Listen to a professor summarize an important discovery. Take notes as you listen. Then use your notes to write short answers to the questions. 🔊

1. When did William Saturno discover the first site? ___20 Years ago___

2. Why was Saturno feeling disappointed? ___he hadn't find something new or exciting___

3. Who probably made the hole that he climbed into? ___an animal___

4. What did he discover in the hole? ___Paintings nearly 2000 Years old___

5. Where was the second site, Guatemala or somewhere else? ___Guatemala___

Part of the Maya murals discovered by William Saturno in San Bartolo, Guatemala

D Think about something you discovered. It could be an object, information, or something else. Prepare to talk about your discovery by making notes in the chart.

What did you discover?	paintings and words in Arabic, more than 100 years
Where or how did you discover it?	on a desers, I found it in a rock
What did you do or what happened after you discovered it?	I search about what language is that and when is written

E Work with a partner. Take turns talking about the thing you found using your notes from exercise D. When it is your turn to listen, take notes about what you hear.

F **SUMMARIZE** Work with a different partner. Summarize the talk you heard in exercise E using your notes. | Critical Thinking

Review

A **VOCABULARY** Complete the sentences with the correct form of the words from the box. TWO words are extra.

ancient	demonstration	interpret	purpose	site
civilization	imagine	preserve	sign up	volunteer

Uxmal is an archaeological ¹_____ in Mexico. It is an important and

²_____ Maya city. The Maya ³_____ survived for thousands of years.

Visitors to Uxmal can ⁴_____ to take a tour. The tour guide's job is to

⁵_____ things for them. The buildings at Uxmal are beautiful. Many have been

⁶_____ well. There is also a large open court there. The ⁷_____ of this

court was to play ball games. Visiting Uxmal is interesting. You can ⁸_____ what

life was like in Maya times.

B **GRAMMAR** Rewrite these sentences about Uxmal using infinitives of purpose.

1. People go to Uxmal because they are interested in seeing an ancient Maya city.

   _____

2. Some visitors to Uxmal hire a tour guide. They want to learn more about the site.

   _____

3. Uxmal had a large open court that the Maya used for playing ball games.

   _____

C **PRONUNCIATION** Practice reading aloud the information in exercise A. Use natural sentence stress.

D **SPEAKING SKILL** Choose ONE of these topics. Summarize what you remember about it.

- Minseok Folk Village
- Colonial Williamsburg
- Doggerland

RE-ASSESS What skills or language still need improvement?

Final Tasks

OPTION 1   Discuss special objects from your past

A   Look at the photo and read the caption. Discuss with a partner what you can infer about Emma from the objects that are special to her?

B   **BRAINSTORM**   Make a list of objects that are special to you. They could be objects from your past that you have special memories of or objects that have been useful or important to you over the years.

C   Work in a group. Take turns sharing objects from your list in exercise B. When it is your turn to speak, say what objects you have chosen and why they are special to you. When it is your turn to listen, ask questions to find out more about the special objects.

D   Share the most memorable objects you heard about with the class. Discuss what future generations might learn if they discovered your objects.

◀ An image, titled "Emma," from artist Regina Tremmel's "Memento" series about things that are special to people

OPTION 2 Present a historical object, site, or person

A MODEL Listen to a student deliver a talk about a well-known person from history. Complete the notes. 🔊

Who is the talk about?	• Tutankhamun: ancient pharaoh (a kind of ^{1}_____)
Where / when did this person live?	• in Egypt about ^{2}_____ years ago
What did this person do?	• pharaoh for less than ^{3}_____ years
Why is this person well-known?	Three things happened after his death:
	• lots of ^{4}_____ objects were put in his tomb
	• treasure still there when it was found in ^{5}_____
	• radio stations and ^{6}_____ spread the story
What do people think now?	• Tutankhamun is now important symbol of Egypt

---

PRESENTATION SKILL Consider What Your Listeners Need to Know

Good presenters think about what their listeners do not know and then give that information. In other words, they imagine which basic facts are important but may not be known. They also think of what questions their listeners might want to ask beyond the basic facts and answer those questions, too. Doing this makes it easier for listeners to understand the key ideas.

B ANALYZE THE MODEL Listen again. Number the information the speaker gives in the order each point is mentioned. 🔊

a. _____ What objects were put with Tutankhamun's body

b. _____ What the word "pharaoh" means

c. _____ What the word "tomb" means

d. _____ When Tutankhamun was pharaoh and for how long

e. _____ When Tutankhamun's body was discovered

f. _____ Why newspapers wrote about the discovery of Tutankhamun's tomb

C PLAN After you decide which historical object, site, or person you will talk about, complete the steps.

1. Make notes about what you will say about this topic. Describe why it is important to study today. Do some research if you wish.

2. Decide what listeners need to know about your topic and organize your notes so your presentation will be clear.

D PRACTICE AND PRESENT Practice giving your presentation with a partner before you present it to the class.

SPECIES SURVIVAL 9

A red fox searches for food in a garbage can in London, England.

IN THIS UNIT, YOU WILL:

- Watch or listen to a talk about protecting endangered species
- Watch a video on chameleon adaptation
- Listen to a discussion about dealing with mosquitoes
- Design a poster to protect a plant or animal
  OR Present on an endangered species with a partner

THINK AND DISCUSS:

1. What wild animals can you see around cities in your country?
2. What do species that survive in cities have in common?
3. Do you think people do enough to help other species survive? Why or why not?

Look at the information. Then answer the questions.

1. How do these animal survival stories make you feel?

2. What human actions helped the animals represented in the photos?

3. Why do people seem to care about some animals more than others?

HUMANS and ANIMALS

Otters almost became extinct in Singapore in the 1970s because of pollution and deforestation. But in the late 1990s, they started returning to the island because of the effects of the government's clean-up campaign. Their population continues to grow.

Development and overfishing in Baja California, Mexico, threaten to destroy the natural wonders people come to see, such as the gray whales. In contrast, ecotourism brings in hundreds of millions of dollars to Mexico and helps support both the residents and the animals.

Gray wolves were reintroduced into Yellowstone National Park in Wyoming, USA, during the late 1990s, after they were completely killed off in the 1920s. Their population has fully recovered now, and they help to balance life in the park.

A Vocabulary

A **MEANING FROM CONTEXT** Listen and think about the meaning of the words in blue. Then write each word next to its definition on the next page. 🔊

SPECIES IN DANGER

Species go **extinct** for many reasons. For example, if the climate gets colder and some plants cannot grow, **creatures** that **depend on** these plants for food could die out. Natural disasters are another reason. Research shows that volcanoes caused the deaths of many species **approximately** 200 million years ago.

Humans also cause species to die out. Sometimes we are **directly** the reason: Passenger pigeons went extinct—the last one died on exactly September 1, 1914—because people ate so many of them. In other **cases**, we are indirectly the cause. For example, people brought animals like pigs and monkeys to the only island where dodo birds lived. As a **consequence**, these birds went extinct because the pigs and monkeys ate their food and eggs.

However, it isn't all bad news; there are survival successes, too. For example, scientists sometimes find "extinct" species are actually still alive. Take the Bolivian Cochran frog, also known as the glass frog. Scientists thought it was extinct, but researchers found some in 2020. The **endangered** animals were taken to a special center, where they are **currently** being kept safe.

And some people have made it their **mission** to protect endangered species. In the past, huge numbers of *Pau Brasil* trees were cut down. However, the *Pau Brasil* is Brazil's national tree and important in that country's history. People all over the country wanted to save it, so they protected older trees and planted new ones.

Bolivian Cochran frog

1. _____ (adj) in danger

2. _____ (adj) no longer alive

3. _____ (adv) about or roughly

4. _____ (adv) at this time

5. _____ (adv) with nothing else involved

6. _____ (n) a particular situation

7. _____ (n) a result, especially a negative one

8. _____ (n) an important goal or purpose in life

9. _____ (n) any living thing except a plant

10. _____ (v phr) to need something for support or help

VOCABULARY SKILL   Antonyms

Antonyms are words that have opposite meanings. Antonyms can be single words
or phrases. Learning antonyms can help you build your vocabulary so you can better
understand others and express your ideas.

alive—dead	*preserve—destroy*
ancient—modern	*take part in—withdraw from*

B Match the words to their antonyms in the box.

alive	exactly	in the past	indirectly	safe	survive

1. approximately—_____

2. currently—_____

3. directly—_____

4. endangered—_____

5. extinct—_____

6. go extinct—_____

C Work with a partner. Choose five words from the text in exercise A that have antonyms you
know, such as *many—few*. Share your ideas with the class.

D **PERSONALIZE** In a group, discuss these questions. Support your opinions.

1. Think of a recent decision you made. What have been some **consequences** of it?

2. When you were younger, who did you mainly **depend on** for advice?

3. What are some things you like about the place where you're **currently** living?

4. Is there any kind of **creature** you dislike? Why? What might happen if it went **extinct**?

A Listening Protecting Endangered Creatures

Critical Thinking

A **ACTIVATE** Work in a group. Look at the photo and read the caption. Then discuss the questions.

1. Why does the sign say "Missing" and "Have you seen me?"
2. What does "Reward: Survival" mean?
3. How likely is it that the sign will get people's attention?

B **MAIN IDEAS** Watch or listen and take notes. Then decide whether each statement is about Lucy Cooke or Joel Sartore. Write *L* for Lucy, *J* for Joel, or *B* for both. 🔊 ▶

1. _____ Became interested in animals as a child

2. _____ Feels people need to understand unusual animals

3. _____ Feels photos are a way to help species

4. _____ Started a project to photograph wild animals in human care (i.e., at zoos, aquariums, and wildlife parks)

5. _____ Wants to teach people about wild animals

▼ An informative sign at the preview of *Missing,* an exhibition by artist and environmentalist Louis Masai in London, England

DETAILS Listen again. Complete the notes with ONE word or a number that the speaker says. 🔊

UN Report	Earth: 8 million species (about ¹_____ million endangered) All species depend on other species e.g., people depend on ²_____ / insects for food crops

Animals	Species like elephants, ³_____, giant pandas not likely to go extinct
	
	    ↑ popular / loved so people would try to save them
	
	Less popular / attractive creatures need protection
	
	    e.g., proboscis monkey or Titicaca water ⁴_____

Lucy Cooke	Does many things to help animals:
	
	    e.g., gives ⁵_____, writes books, hosts shows, makes documentaries, and takes photos
	
	Says animals not ugly: how they look depends on where and how they live
	
	    e.g., blobfish look different in tanks than at bottom of ⁶_____

Joel Sartore	Became sad when learned certain ⁷_____ species were extinct Started Photo Ark project to get people to care about endangered animals = plans to photograph about ⁸_____ species of animals

NOTE-TAKING SKILL   Review Your Notes

Revising your notes after class can help you understand and remember key ideas. You can:

- Add information you remember that you did not note while listening.
- Delete notes that seem unnecessary because they are not about key ideas.
- Check answers to questions you had or confirm information that you did not understand.
- Organize your notes using a graphic organizer such as an outline, spider map, Venn diagram, or time line.
- Write a summary of the key ideas; it will be helpful when you need to study.

D Organize the notes in exercise C into a spider map with "Endangered Species" at the center. Compare your spider map with a partner.

E **FOCUSED LISTENING** Work with a partner. Discuss what words could be antonyms of each word below. Then listen to the excerpts to confirm your answers. 🔊

1. strange—_____

2. black—_____

3. cute—_____

4. different—_____

A Speaking

A RECALL In Listening A, you heard about the views of two National Geographic Explorers. Discuss the questions in a group.

1. Lucy Cooke believes that people need to understand strange or unusual-looking animals better in order to care about them and protect them. Do you agree with this view?

2. Joel Sartore feels that taking pictures of animals against a black or white background lets us see them clearly. It also allows us to look the animals in the eyes and feel like we're having a "conversation" with them. Do you agree with this view?

PRONUNCIATION   Thought Groups

🔊 We divide the words we say into *thought groups*. These are words or ideas that naturally go together, such as phrases, clauses, or even short sentences. After each thought group, we usually pause briefly. And the last content word of each thought group is usually stressed.

*Like Lucy **Cooke**, / Explorer Joel **Sartore** / also became interested in **animals** / as a **child**.*

B Read the opinions about animals. Decide how to divide them into thought groups. Then work with a partner and take turns saying them.

1. Research shows that animals think and feel and have different personalities, so we need to make sure every animal can live a good life.

2. Animals have families, just like people do. So we should treat animals as well as we treat our families.

3. Just leave wild animals alone. Taking selfies with them is dangerous for everyone.

4. It's OK for animals to be food for humans. People have eaten animals for millions of years.

▼ Long-tailed macaques on a beach in Khao Sam Roi Yot National Park, Thailand

CRITICAL THINKING   Evaluate the Strength of Ideas

To decide whether an idea is strong or weak, ask yourself how good the speaker's support is.

Strong ideas are supported by facts or evidence that you can trust. Weak ideas are often too general. They may be unsupported, supported by opinions only, or supported by information that may be incorrect.

Note that a point may be strong even if you disagree with it. And a point may be weak even if you agree with it.

C Work in a group. Consider the opinions in exercise B. Which ones do you agree with? Do you know of any facts or evidence to support these opinions. | Critical Thinking

D **ANALYZE** Work with a partner. Discuss whether zoos are beneficial for animals. Think of facts or evidence to support your ideas. | Critical Thinking

SPEAKING SKILL   Express Cause and Effect

Causes are the reasons why something happens. Effects are the results of an event or situation.

To introduce a cause, use expressions like *because, since*, or *the reason is (that)*:
   Elephants will probably not go extinct. Why? **Because** *they're very popular.*

To introduce an effect, use expressions like *so, as a result, therefore,* or *as a consequence.*
   Elephants are very popular. **Therefore,** *they will probably not go extinct.*

You can also use an *if* clause to show a cause-effect relationship.
   If *animals are not protected, they may become endangered.*

E Underline the expressions that introduce causes or effects. Then say the sentences using natural thought groups.

1. Giraffes can eat leaves that are up high. The reason is that they have long necks.
2. Colors can help birds find a partner, so male birds of some species are very colorful.
3. Their light fur makes polar bears hard to notice. As a result, they can catch food easily.
4. Chameleons can be hard to see because they can change the color of their skin.
5. If glaciers keep melting, polar bears will lose their habitat.

F Work with a partner. Rewrite the cause and effect expressions in exercise E with the expressions in parentheses. Take turns saying the new sentences with natural thought groups.

1. (as a result) _____

2. (because) _____

3. (since) _____

4. (so) _____

5. (as a consequence) _____

Critical Thinking | **G** **IDENTIFY** Work with a partner. Look at the infographic and complete the tasks.

1. Identify each of the animals in the infographic.
2. Think of other examples of creatures from THREE of the categories.
3. Share your examples with another pair of students. Can they identify which categories your examples fit in?

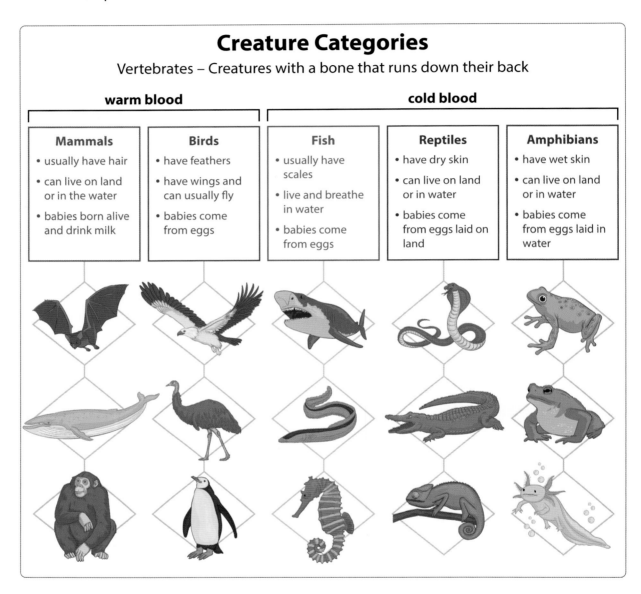

Creature Categories

Vertebrates – Creatures with a bone that runs down their back

warm blood		cold blood		
Mammals	**Birds**	**Fish**	**Reptiles**	**Amphibians**
• usually have hair • can live on land or in the water • babies born alive and drink milk	• have feathers • have wings and can usually fly • babies come from eggs	• usually have scales • live and breathe in water • babies come from eggs	• have dry skin • can live on land or in water • babies come from eggs laid on land	• have wet skin • can live on land or in water • babies come from eggs laid in water

Critical Thinking | **H** **ANALYZE** Work with a partner. Complete the tasks.

1. Choose a creature from one of the categories that you think is endangered.
2. Discuss what has caused your chosen creature to become endangered; for example, being killed by humans or other species (for food or another reason), climate change, diseases, losing their homes because of humans or other species, pollution.
3. Imagine that your chosen creature became extinct. Discuss what some of the possible effects might be on both people and other species.

Amazing Chameleons

alteration (n) the act of changing something
background (n) everything behind something
camouflage (n) behavior or appearance that allows one
　　　　　to hide
charismatic (adj) having traits that attract people

diversity (n) variety
mimic (v) to copy
predator (n) an animal that eats another animal
rotating (adj) moving in a circle

▲ Veiled chameleons, like this
one, are native to Saudi Arabia.

A **ACTIVATE** Read the definitions of words from the video. Then discuss how these words relate | Critical Thinking
to chameleons.

B Read the statements. Then watch the video. Number the ideas in the order you hear them. ▶

a. _____ Chameleons move like leaves or branches that are blowing in the wind.

b. _____ Female chameleons may change color to tell males they are not interested.

c. _____ One way chameleons communicate with each other is to change color.

d. _____ The main problem for chameleons is that their homes are being destroyed.

C Watch again. Complete the statements with the numbers you hear. ▶

1. There are _____ species of chameleon. Of these, _____ percent
live on Madagascar.

2. Scientists discovered information about the skin of chameleons in the year _____.

3. Chameleons can project, or throw forward, their tongues up to _____ body
lengths at approximately 5.8 meters per second (or _____ miles per hour).

4. About _____ percent of chameleon species are in danger of going extinct.
In addition, _____ species are considered critically endangered, and
_____ species are endangered.

B Vocabulary

A **MEANING FROM CONTEXT** Work with a partner. Read and listen to the conversations. Notice the words in blue and think about their meanings. 🔊

Andy:	My sister's trying to **convince** me to stop eating meat.
Bo-Sang:	That doesn't seem **realistic**. I mean, she knows how much you love meat. Still, eating plants more often *would* be good for the planet.
Andy:	Yeah, she said that meat production is a **threat** to the environment. I guess I'll **consider** it.
Carly:	You're writing a story for your creative writing class? Cool! What's it about?
Deanna:	Well, this **deadly** illness is **spreading** across the country. A doctor starts developing a medicine to **cure** it. She makes a lot of **progress**, but then she catches the disease and dies before she can tell anyone about the cure!
Carly:	Sounds exciting . . . but also kind of sad!
Eduardo:	Argh! My new computer must have a virus. I've tried to **get rid of** it, but nothing works. It's been like this since I bought it, and I haven't been able to do any work.
Fatima:	Well, return it. You paid for it, so you have the **right** to a computer that works.
Eduardo:	Yeah, you're right. I'll do that.

B Complete each definition with the correct form of a word from exercise A.

1. _____ (adj) understanding and accepting what is real and likely

2. _____ (adj) very dangerous and likely to kill

3. _____ (n) improvement, positive development, or forward movement

4. _____ (n) something or someone that could cause damage or harm

5. _____ (n) the ability to have or get something or to act a certain way

6. _____ (v phr) to remove something you do not want

7. _____ (v) to make a sick person healthy again

8. _____ (v) to pass or communicate something to many people

9. _____ (v) to persuade someone to do or believe something

10. _____ (v) to spend time thinking about something

C Take the quiz. Check T for *True* or F for *False*. Then listen to check the answers. Who knows the most about mosquitoes in the class? 🔊

Mosquito Quiz

Mosquitoes! Most people hate them, and it's obvious why: They bite. They carry diseases. And if one's in your room at night, don't even **consider** trying to sleep before you've **gotten rid of** it! Still, is everything about these tiny insects negative? Take the quiz and find out. Perhaps it will **convince** you that they're not all bad!

1 There are approximately 3500 species of mosquitos in the world.

☐ T ☐ F

2 If a female mosquito is buzzing around you, don't worry. Only males bite.

☐ T ☐ F

3 All species of mosquitoes **spread** diseases that affect people.

☐ T ☐ F

4 Mosquitoes can be dangerous to people, but sharks are a much bigger **threat**.

☐ T ☐ F

5 Malaria can be **deadly**, but it doesn't kill many people each year.

☐ T ☐ F

6 Even though we have seen a lot of scientific **progress** recently, it's **realistic** to think it would take scientists many years to **cure** malaria.

☐ T ☐ F

7 In some countries, people believe mosquitoes have the **right** to bite you.

☐ T ☐ F

D **PERSONALIZE** Discuss the questions with a group.

1. How do you feel about mosquitoes?
2. How much of a problem are mosquitoes in your country?
3. What should people do about the problem of mosquitoes?

B Listening Solving the Mosquito Problem

Critical Thinking | **A** **PREDICT** You will hear a discussion about how people might be able to deal with mosquitoes. Which FOUR of these ideas do you think the speakers will discuss?

   a. Mosquitoes spread diseases; one solution would be to get rid of all of them.
   b. The most effective way to deal with mosquitoes is for people to use nets.
   c. It would be hard, expensive, and maybe impossible to kill all mosquitoes.
   d. There's no way to solve the mosquito problem; people just have to live with them.
   e. Improving and saving human lives is more important than protecting insects.
   f. Killing all mosquitoes would be very likely to have negative consequences.
   g. People failed to kill mosquitoes in the past, so it is unlikely to work in the future.

B **MAIN IDEAS** Listen to the discussion and take notes in the chart. Use your notes to confirm your answers in exercise A. 🔊

Dr. Habib (biologist)	Dr. Pereira (ecologist)	Dr. Sharma (medical doctor)

▼ A bird hunts and eats mosquitoes.

C **DETAILS** Listen again and add to your notes. Then match the ideas to the person who expresses them. Write H for *Dr. Habib*, P for *Dr. Pereira*, or S for *Dr. Sharma*. 🔊

1. _____ A way to kill off one kind of mosquito is unlikely to work on other kinds.

2. _____ In the 1960s, scientists got rid of a species of insect that affected cows.

3. _____ Killing all mosquitoes would surely have negative consequences.

4. _____ It's a good thing that scientists killed off the smallpox virus back in the 1970s.

5. _____ It's not realistic to think the diseases that mosquitoes spread can be cured.

6. _____ Many species, including birds and frogs, depend on mosquitoes for food.

7. _____ There are 3500 species of mosquitoes, but only about 100 spread diseases.

8. _____ We need to deal with mosquitoes, but killing them all is not the right solution.

See Critical Thinking Skill in this unit.

LISTENING SKILL   **Recognize Opinions and Facts**

Opinions are ideas that some people believe are true, but which other people may not agree with. In contrast, facts are true and can be checked.

> **Opinion:** *Chameleons are ugly.*   **Fact:** *Chameleons can change color.*

Recognizing opinions and facts can help you decide how strong a speaker's arguments are. Listen for adjectives, adverbs, and phrases that signal opinions.

> *It's a **beautiful/ugly** animal.*
>
> *We will **definitely/never** be able to save all animals from extinction.*
>
> *I **think/For me**, mosquitoes are just a part of life we have to deal with.*

D Work with a partner. Look at the ideas in exercise C. Match them to the correct category. Then discuss which opinions you agree with and why.

Opinions	Facts
1	

E Use your notes to match these causes and effects. Then listen to the excerpts to confirm your answers. 🔊

1. If humans got rid of all mosquitoes, it's possible _____

2. If humans killed disease-spreading mosquitoes, maybe _____

3. Scientists got rid of a disease in the 1970s and now _____

4. If people improved education and housing, then _____

a. birds and other species would not have enough to eat.

b. it might save more lives than killing off all mosquitoes.

c. people can no longer die from catching the smallpox virus.

d. mosquito species that are safe now might start spreading deadly diseases.

B Speaking

Critical Thinking

A **RECALL** In Listening B, you heard a discussion about whether people should get rid of mosquitoes, a creature that many dislike. Work in a group to complete these steps.

1. Make a list of four creatures: one you all love, one you all like, one none of you mind, and one you all hate.

2. Join another group. Share your list of creatures in order from largest to smallest. Can the students in the other group guess which one you love, like, don't mind, and hate?

GRAMMAR FOR SPEAKING   Adverbs and Modals of Possibility and Necessity

Adverbs to express possibility

We can use adverbs to say how likely, or possible, something is.

more unlikely ← → more likely

definitely not   probably not   possibly   probably   definitely/certainly

> People will **possibly/probably/definitely** do more to save animals in the future.
> We **probably** won't see any sharks in the water around here.

Modals to express possibility

We use *may, might,* and *could* + base verb to say something is possible.

> I think people **may/might/could** do more to save animals in the future.

Expressing necessity

We use *must* and semi-modals + base verb to say something is necessary.

> We **must protect** endangered animals or they will go extinct.
> We'**ve got to/have to/need to save** endangered animals.

B Underline the adverbs and modals of possibility and necessity in this conversation.

A: I finally found a new apartment, but I don't have a car, and, well . . .
B: You'd like some help moving? Of course. I can probably help you. When?

A: I need to move in before next Thursday, so how does Monday sound?
B: My parents said they want to visit on Monday. They might change their minds, but . . .

A: OK then, what about Tuesday?
B: Anya and I may be going to a movie.

A: So, Wednesday? Please say yes!
B: Wednesday? Yeah, Wednesday! Possibly.

A: Possibly? Why Possibly? I need definitely!
B: Wednesdays are usually busy, so I've probably forgotten something I must do.

A: Argh! I guess I'll have to ask somebody else.

C Match the sentences to make short conversations.

1. A: There are only two northern white rhinoceroses left in the world and they're both female.
   B: _____

2. A: My son told me he doesn't want to go to the zoo anymore because wild animals should be free.
   B: _____

3. A: I'll see you at the river-cleaning meeting at three this afternoon.
   B: _____

4. A: Did you know that sea turtles have been around for more than one hundred million years?
   B: _____

5. A: I heard you saw that new wildlife documentary. What did you think?
   B: _____

a. He's probably becoming more aware about animals and their rights.
b. OK. I have class until 2:30, so I might be a little late.
c. Really? I think the species will definitely go extinct then.
d. Wow! Their ancestors probably swam with dinosaurs.
e. You've got to see it. It's really inspiring.

D Work with a partner to complete the sentences.

1. Before we decide to get rid of mosquitoes, we'll need to . . .
2. If we really want to save animals, we have to . . .
3. To make sure humans don't become an endangered species, we definitely need to . . .
4. If we want to work to protect wildlife, we might possibly need to . . .
5. Before getting a pet, we'll need to . . .

◀ A giant panda eats bamboo at Zoo Atlanta in the United States.

Review

SELF-ASSESS

How well can you . . .?	Very well.	OK.	I need improvement.
use the key vocabulary	☐	☐	☐
use thought groups	☐	☐	☐
talk about causes and effects	☐	☐	☐
use adverbs and modals of possibility and necessity	☐	☐	☐

A **VOCABULARY** Choose the correct words.

Unfortunately, humans can be ¹(creatures / threats) to other animals. Some species have even gone ²(extinct / realistic) as a ³(consequence / mission) of our actions. And ⁴(approximately / currently), many more are ⁵(deadly / endangered). A lot of people believe this is wrong. Some of them, such as National Geographic Explorers Lucy Cooke and Joel Sartore, are working to bring more attention to animals and their ⁶(mission / right) to live safely. Will they make ⁷(a case / progress) and be successful, or will more species die out? The answer ⁸(considers / depends on) the choices and actions of us all.

B **PRONUNCIATION** Decide how to divide the sentences in exercise A into thought groups. Practice saying the sentences.

C **GRAMMAR** Answer the questions with expressions of possibility or necessity.

1. What is one thing you will probably do tomorrow?
2. Who is one person you might talk to later today?
3. Where is one place you have to visit soon?
4. What is one thing you need to do now that you didn't have to do as a child?
5. What will likely happen to animals that lose their habitat?

D **SPEAKING SKILL** Think of something great that happened to you when you were younger. Discuss what caused it and what some of its effects were.

RE-ASSESS What skills or language still need improvement?

Final Tasks

OPTION 1 Design a poster to protect a plant or animal

A Work with a partner. Look at the posters. Discuss the questions.

  1. What does the message on each poster mean? Use a dictionary if necessary.
  2. Which poster do you think has the most powerful message and why?

Frogs and toads are **dying**. We can't just let them croak!

Your choices:
1. Protect endangered species
2. Lose them forever

Bees are endangered. If we don't save them, so is our **food!**

Millions of other species share our home. Why don't we act like it?

B Work with a small group. Decide which plant or animal you want to preserve and why. Then come up with a powerful message to get people in your community to take action to preserve it.

C With the same group, design your poster with your message on it. Add a picture or photo if you wish. Then present your ideas to the class: Say which plant or animal you think it is important to save, and share your poster and explain its message.

▼ People protest for the protection of the climate and environment, which all plants and animals need.

OPTION 2 Present on an endangered species

A MODEL Listen to two students deliver a talk about an animal that is under threat. Complete the notes. 🔊

What animal do they talk about?	•
Why is this creature endangered?	• – –
How can people protect this animal?	• • • • •

PRESENTATION SKILL Mention Your Sources

When you deliver a presentation, mention the research you did and the sources you used. This can make your arguments stronger. Use phrases like:

> *"According to my professor, . . ."*
>
> *"The* New York Times *says that . . ."*
>
> *"I read in* National Geographic *magazine that . . ."*

Remember to use sources you can depend on and that are not out of date. For online sources, choose sites such as reputable newspapers or educational institutions. Sites for entertainment or sites where people express personal opinions may not always have correct information.

B ANALYZE THE MODEL Listen again. Which speaker does each thing? Write M for *man*, W for *woman*, or B for *both*. 🔊

1. _____ Describes possible solutions

2. _____ Explains who will say what

3. _____ Expresses personal opinions

4. _____ Mentions research sources

5. _____ Repeats their partner's point

6. _____ Talks about causes or effects

C PLAN Work with a partner to complete the steps.

1. Decide which endangered species you will talk about.
2. Research why this species is endangered and how we could protect it. Suggest ways your community can take action to help the species.
3. Plan what you will say in each part of the talk and who will say it.

D PRACTICE AND PRESENT Practice giving your presentation with your partner before you present it to the class.

FINDING SUCCESS 10

Gnanli Landrou is a young entrepreneur from Togo. He developed a technology that produces ecological concrete for building houses.

IN THIS UNIT, YOU WILL:

- Watch or listen to a talk about how to be successful
- Watch a video on a social entrepreneur
- Listen to a discussion about people who break the rules
- Discuss different kinds of success
  OR Present on a failure that became a success

THINK AND DISCUSS:

1. Which of your family members or friends would you describe as successful? Why?

2. What is something you would like to succeed at?

3. Does success depend more on hard work or creativity?

Look at the information. Then answer the questions.

1. What are some language-based tasks that you do every day?

2. What are some challenges that Steven Spielberg might face because of his dyslexia?

3. Why is creativity important in business?

Dyslexia and Creativity

People with dyslexia find it hard to read fluently and spell words correctly. They learn to manage language-based tasks in creative ways. In fact, researchers at the University of Cambridge in England found that people with dyslexia are especially good at discovery, invention, and creativity.

Award-winning American filmmaker Steven Spielberg has plenty of creative vision. He also has dyslexia. School was tough for him. He got into filmmaking when he was twelve and says, "Making movies was my great escape."

Seven of Spielberg's movies, including *Jurassic Park*, are part of the National Film Registry in the United States, which preserves films that are culturally, historically, and artistically important.

Steven Spielberg, who directed the 1993 film *Jurassic Park*, sits between a pair of giant dinosaur feet in a photo to promote the film. *Jurassic Park* made more money than any other movie had made up to that time.

A Vocabulary

A Listen and repeat. Check the words you know. 🔊

ambition (n)	**complain** (v)	**determination** (n)	**flexible** (adj)	**income** (n)
characteristic (n)	**confidence** (n)	**doubt** (n)	**give up** (v phr)	**lack** (v)

B **MEANING FROM CONTEXT** Listen and write the words you hear. Then think about their meanings. 🔊

DIFFERENT TYPES OF ENTREPRENEURS

Entrepreneurs typically share certain ¹_____. For example, they have the ²_____ to work hard and the ³_____ to succeed. They are ⁴_____ and can adapt to changing business situations. And they can overcome their own ⁵_____ and those of others. Many kinds of entrepreneurs are recognized. Their names typically explain what they do.

Social entrepreneurs want to make money and help society. Ecopreneurs are a specific kind of social entrepreneur and want to protect the planet. For example, they might sell products that are environmentally friendly.

As the name suggests, infopreneurs generate ⁶_____ by selling information. An infopreneur might teach an online course about baking cakes, designing websites, or learning English. Computers make selling information easy, so many infopreneurs are also techpreneurs.

Solopreneurs found, or start, their businesses alone. Some have ⁷_____ they can succeed without help. Some might have a business so small that they don't need help. Or others may have no partners because starting a business was accidental. That is, they did not plan to do it.

Wantrepreneurs are different. They talk about wanting to become entrepreneurs but rarely achieve their goal because talking is all they do. In other words, wantrepreneurs don't ⁸_____ on their dream, they never even try to achieve it. This could be because they ⁹_____ the skills or determination to succeed or because they ¹⁰_____ about issues instead of dealing with them.

C Choose the correct word to complete each definition.

1. Ambition means having a strong wish to (be / do) well.
2. Being flexible means (changing / getting upset) if the situation changes.
3. Characteristics are typical (choices / qualities) of a person.
4. Confidence is the feeling that you will (fail / succeed).
5. Determination is the (ability / desire) to keep trying.
6. Doubts are (hopes / worries) about how good something is.
7. Income is how much money a person (earns / spends).
8. To complain about a thing is to say it is (right / wrong).
9. To give up means to stop (doing or trying / having or sharing) something.
10. To lack something means to not (believe / have) it.

D Work with a partner to complete the word-form table. Use a dictionary if necessary.

	Noun	Verb	Adjective
1	ambition	_ _ _ _ _ _ _	
2		complain	_ _ _ _ _ _ _ _
3	doubt		
4			flexible
5		lack	

VOCABULARY SKILL   Word Blends

New words are sometimes created by mixing, or blending, parts of other words. If you recognize the meanings of the blended words, you can understand the new words.

Original word	Original word	Blend
education	entertainment	edutainment
breakfast	lunch	brunch

If you know *education* and *entertainment*, you can guess that *edutainment* is probably educational entertainment.

And if you know *breakfast* and *lunch*, you can guess that *brunch* is a meal between breakfast and lunch.

E With a partner, discuss what the names of the entrepreneurs in the text in exercise B are a blend of. Then discuss what these words mean: *infomercial*, *webinar*, *staycation*.

F Work with a group to make up some new word blends or search for some online. Share them with the class. Can other students guess which words were blended and the meanings of the new words?

A Listening Five Things You Need to Succeed

Critical Thinking | **A** **PREDICT** You will hear a talk about five things you need to succeed in business. Discuss with a partner some things you think the speaker might mention.

B **MAIN IDEAS** Watch or listen and check the main points you hear. THREE points are extra. 🔊 ▶

1. _____ Being popular and attractive is more important than being good at what you do.

2. _____ Even if you lack money or a business plan, you can still start a successful business.

3. _____ When you start a business, it's OK if you or others have doubts about its success.

4. _____ Many people who are now successful entrepreneurs did not finish their education.

5. _____ Ask for advice only from successful people or people who helped you in the past.

6. _____ Not everyone has an ambition to be an entrepreneur; sometimes it just happens.

7. _____ It's good to have determination, not give up, and be flexible when things change.

8. _____ Accept that you can't solve every problem or know the answer to every question.

9. _____ Work as much as possible during the first year that your company is in business.

10. _____ Having confidence in yourself and a good sense of humor can both be very helpful.

C **DETAILS** Listen again and complete the notes about the people mentioned in the talk. 🔊

People	Companies	Facts
Sergey Brin and Larry Page	1 _____	Started their company without having a 2 _____
Do Won Chang	3 _____	Worked in gas stations and 4 _____ before starting the company
Mikaila Ulmer	Me & the Bees Lemonade	Started a business, which gives money to 5 _____ bees, when she was just four
Qunfei Zhou	Lens Technology	Did not finish 6 _____ but started a company that is now a leader in making glass 7 _____
Melissa Kieling	PackIt	Started her business after her 8 _____ complained about their school lunches

Sergey Brin (left) and Larry Page (right) play with Legos, one of their favorite toys, during a break at a sales conference.

LISTENING SKILL   Recognize Humor

Some speakers use humor when they talk to help make their points fun and memorable. This can involve telling jokes, saying something funny, using humorous gestures or tone of voice, or even saying the opposite of what they really mean.

Noticing when speakers are trying to be funny can help you better understand their message. It can also help you decide how to react to their words. For example, if you recognize someone is being humorous, you know not to take their statements too seriously.

D **PERSONALIZE** Discuss the questions with a group.

1. At what point did you recognize that the speaker of "Five Things You Need to Succeed" was being humorous? Was it before or after she said, "Well, I was joking, of course"?

2. Which form of humor did the speaker mainly use: telling jokes, saying funny things, using a humorous tone of voice, or saying the opposite of what she really meant?

3. How funny did you find the talk: very funny, kind of funny, or not funny? Why?

4. Would you use humor in a talk? Why or why not?

E **ANALYZE** Sergey Brin and Larry Page used humor to create a relaxed and fun environment for employees at Google. What rules do you think leaders and employees should follow when using humor at work?

Critical Thinking

Speaking

CRITICAL THINKING   Categorize

When you categorize, you put things with similar characteristics together into the same category or group. For example, stores can be categorized as grocery stores, convenience stores, specialty stores, discount stores, etc. Each category has its unique characteristics. When you understand the characteristics of each group, you can put items in the appropriate category. Categorizing is an important skill for school, work, and life because organized information is easier to understand and remember.

Critical Thinking | **A** Decide which characteristics below are likely or unlikely to affect how successful a person is and write them in the chart.

attractive	funny	married	slim
bright	healthy	polite	strong
female	lazy	popular	tall
friendly	lucky	rich	young

Likely to affect a person's success	Unlikely to affect a person's success

▼ A mompreneur working while taking care of a baby at home

B Compare your ideas from exercise A with a partner. Discuss and explain your views.

GRAMMAR FOR SPEAKING   Adverbs of Degree

We use adverbs of degree to make an idea stronger or weaker. Common examples include *especially, extremely, kind of, particularly, quite, (not) really, so,* and *(not) very.*

Adverbs of degree can modify adjectives:

> It was **extremely** / **not very** / **really** good.

They can also modify other adverbs:

> They did it **especially** / **quite** / **so** quickly.

Some adverbs of degree (but usually not *extremely, so,* or *very*) can modify certain verbs.

> She **particularly** / **really** enjoyed working at that company.

In most cases, we put adverbs of degree before the word or information they modify.

C   Listen to some excerpts from the talk. Write the adverbs of degree that you hear. 🔊

1. Sergey Brin and Larry Page didn't have a business plan, and their business has been
   _____ successful.

2. It worked, and Kieling ended up starting a business called PackIt, which is
   _____ successful.

3. That's not to say that achieving business success is _____ easy. It's not, and in
   fact, there are five characteristics entrepreneurs do need. And I'm not joking this time.

4. You may fail along the way—most people do. But if you give up, it's _____
   unlikely that you'll succeed.

5. And finally, well, I find that it _____ helps to have a good sense of humor!

D   **PERSONALIZE**   Choose the right adverbs. Then answer the questions.

1. What is one sport you (really / very) enjoy playing or watching?
   _____

2. What is one thing you can do (real / really) quickly and well?
   _____

3. What music do you think is (especially good / good especially)?
   _____

4. Which subject do you (not really / not very) want to study?
   _____

5. Where is one place you would (particularly / so) like to visit?
   _____

E   Interview a partner using the questions in exercise D.

SPEAKING SKILL Paraphrase

Paraphrasing means saying something in different words. We often paraphrase to make an idea clearer or to express it more simply.

There are several ways we can paraphrase.

1. Use synonyms (or antonyms) of the words in the original information:

    Don't stop trying! You can still do it. → *Don't give up! You can still make it.*

2. Use the same words as in the original but change their form:

    He had doubts about Jon's confidence. → *He doubted if Jon was confident.*

3. Change the grammar of the original and/or the order of the ideas:

    The business doesn't make enough money. → *The company isn't doing well.*

The most effective approach to paraphrasing is to combine two or three methods.

We sometimes use these expressions when paraphrasing:

    In other words, . . .   *That is, . . .*   *In simpler terms, . . .*

F Work with a partner. Take turns saying each sentence and then rephrasing it.

> *I need to get something to eat. In other words, I'm hungry.*

1. I need to get something to eat.
2. What's your motivation for learning English?
3. Our English teacher knows a lot about grammar.
4. I'm interested in starting my own business.
5. Do you have a lot of self-confidence?
6. I have never been on an airplane.

G You are going to watch a video about National Geographic Explorer Sanga Moses. Read the sentences about him. Work with a partner to paraphrase each one. Share your ideas with another pair of students. How similar are your paraphrases?

1. Sanga Moses grew up in a small village in the western part of Uganda.

   _____

2. Starting in 2005, he worked as an accountant in Kampala, the capital of Uganda.

   _____

3. In 2010, he started a company called Eco-Fuel Africa.

   _____

4. Moses is a social entrepreneur, and he was also named a National Geographic Explorer.

   _____

Eco-Fuel Africa

alternative (adj) another
fuel (n) something people use to produce energy

savings (n) money you have saved

▲ National Geographic Explorer Sanga Moses is on a mission to provide inexpensive cooking energy while improving socioeconomic outcomes and stopping deforestation.

A **PREDICT** Read the statements that paraphrase Sanga Moses's story. Think about the order in which they probably happened and number them from 1 to 5. | Critical Thinking

a. _____ Developing the fuel cost Moses a lot of money, and so he had to sell his furniture.

b. _____ Because of Moses's fuel, many Ugandans—including children—have better lives.

c. _____ Finally, Moses developed a cooking fuel that is both cheaper and better than wood.

d. _____ Moses had an idea for a new fuel that could be used for cooking, so he quit his job.

e. _____ Moses saw that children in Uganda often missed school to carry wood for cooking.

B Watch the video. Confirm the order of events in exercise A. ▶

C Watch again. Complete the statements with the words or numbers you hear. ▶

1. Moses began thinking about cooking fuel when he met his _____ sister crying.

2. Moses asked a _____ for advice about developing his idea.

3. The new fuel is better for the environment and _____ percent cheaper than wood.

4. The fuel saves forests, reduces pollution, and lets more children _____.

B Vocabulary

A MEANING FROM CONTEXT Work with a partner. Read and listen to the information. Notice the words in blue and think about their meanings. 🔊

CHANDA SHROFF

In many industries, being successful generally seems to involve making and selling **goods** as cheaply as possible. Some entrepreneurs, though, have found success by doing things differently. Chanda Shroff is one example.

On a visit to Kutch in northwest India, Shroff saw special saris, the traditional dress worn in India, embroidered[1] by local women using traditional methods. Shroff wanted to help the women who had made them because they were experiencing a drought.[2] And she thought these clothes were so beautiful that other people would find them attractive, too. So she ordered 30 saris and displayed them at an art exhibit in Mumbai. These saris were not a famous **brand**, but Shroff **charged** a lot for them. Despite the high price, people loved them, and they all sold within a few hours.

After seeing how popular these saris were, Shroff began a new **career** as a social entrepreneur. She founded an **organization** called Shrujan. One of its goals was to help Kutch women gain **motivation**, confidence, and **independence** by earning a **fair** price for their work. Another **aim** was to protect the traditional ways of doing things that these women followed.

Shroff died in 2016 after a long life, but her work lives on. In addition to Shrujan, which is now run by Shroff's children, there is a museum called the Living and Learning Design Centre. This institution is the biggest crafts museum in India. Because of everything she did, it's no surprise that the people of Kutch continue to remember and **respect** Chanda Shroff.

---

[1]**embroidered** (adj) decorated with patterns or pictures that are sewn on
[2]**drought** (n) a long period when there is no rain

Colorful Kutch ▶
hand embroidery

B Complete each definition with a word from exercise A.

1. _____ (adj) equal and reasonable for everybody

2. _____ (n) a company or group of people who work together

3. _____ (n) a goal or a result that you want to achieve

4. _____ (n) a name that identifies goods that a specific company sells

5. _____ (n) a strong feeling that you want to do something

6. _____ (n) the ability to live without help from others

7. _____ (n) the job you do, especially over a long period of time

8. _____ (n) things that people or companies sell

9. _____ (v) to ask for an amount of money when you sell something

10. _____ (v) to think in a positive way about somebody

C **EVALUATE** In what ways are Chanda Shroff and Sanga Moses similar? In what ways are they different? Add ideas to the chart. Then discuss with a group. | Critical Thinking

Chanda Shroff	Both	Sanga Moses

D **PERSONALIZE** Work in a group. Discuss the questions. Support your ideas with reasons, details, and examples.

1. At what age do children usually gain **independence** from their parents? Do you think it would be better if they became independent earlier/later?

2. Which do you think is better: to have one **career** for your whole life or to have several different careers?

3. Which **brands** and **goods** do you like and often buy? Are there any brands or goods that you try to avoid buying?

4. In your view, which is more important for achieving your **aims**: working hard or being lucky?

5. Who is someone you **respect** a lot and why?

Critical Thinking | **A** **ACTIVATE** A "rule breaker" is a person who breaks the rules. Discuss these questions in a group.

1. Who are some rule breakers that you know? Why did they break the rules?
2. What are some situations when it might be good to be a rule breaker?
3. Do you think the speakers will discuss rule breakers they respect or not?

B **MAIN IDEAS** Listen and complete the summary statements with the name of the speaker: Pedro, Ali, or Erika. ONE statement is extra.

1. _____ discusses an entrepreneur whose company sold goods that were good for people, animals, and the planet. This company also paid its farmers and producers fairly.

2. _____ shares information about a businessperson who broke the rules in two ways: first, by paying workers well; second, by letting customers stay as long as they wanted.

Yvon Chouinard near his home in Ventura, California, USA

3. _____ summarizes the story of an entrepreneur who broke the rules many times. People at other companies could not understand why this led to so much success.

4. _____ talks about a businessperson who had two careers. During the second career, this person decided to use part of the company's income to protect the environment.

C   DETAILS Listen again. Match the information to the businesspeople. 🔊

a. "1% for the planet"
b. a climber first
c. an accidental entrepreneur
d. an "antipreneur"
e. company given away
f. no animal testing

g. Patagonia
h. Starbucks
i. The Body Shop
j. "third places"
k. workers are "partners"
l. wrote a book

Howard Schultz	Anita Roddick	Yvon Chouinard

D Listen to some excerpts and write the words you hear. Then write each phrase next to its meaning. 🔊

1. In previous classes, we've seen that many businesses seem to _____ . That is, there are typical things that most of them do.

2. I'm going to talk about Howard Schultz. He's the businessman who helped make Starbucks such a _____ .

3. She was one of the first businesspeople to focus on _____ . Instead of paying the cheapest possible price for _____ and goods, she paid a fair price for them.

a. _____ a business or person whose name almost everyone knows

b. _____ basic things like wool or metal that are used to make goods

c. _____ supporting people who make goods by paying fair prices

d. _____ to do the things that you are expected or supposed to do

E   FOCUSED LISTENING Choose a preposition from the box to complete each phrase. Use each preposition only once. TWO are extra. Then listen to confirm your answers. 🔊

about	at	for	of	on	with

1. to talk _____ something

2. good _____ someone

3. to focus _____ something

4. members _____ an organization

B Speaking

Critical Thinking

A **RECALL** In Listening B, you heard about three businesspeople who "broke the rules." In a group, discuss who probably made each comment below: Howard Schultz, Anita Roddick, or Yvon Chouinard. Then discuss what each one means and whether you agree with it.

- "Business . . . should be about public good, not private greed."
- "How you climb a mountain is more important than reaching the top."
- "Success is empty if you arrive at the finish line alone."

B Read the rules for successful entrepreneurs below. In a group, discuss what each rule means and how much you agree with it. Then make up a new rule. Share it with the class. Explain its meaning and why you think it's a good rule to follow.

- Don't try to do everything alone.
- Saving money is better than spending it.
- Work smarter, not harder.

PRONUNCIATION **Stress for Contrast**

🔊 We usually stress the last content word in each thought group.

*The store sells **clothes**.*
*The entrepreneur achieved her **aim**.*

Sometimes, however, we stress different words to emphasize a contrast. This can be to contrast two ideas or to suggest that some information was incorrect. This stress for contrast, or contrastive stress, is often stronger than stress in normal speech.

*The store only sells **cheap** goods / not **expensive** ones.*
*Actually, / the entrepreneur **didn't** achieve her aim.*

C Underline the words in this conversation that would be stressed for contrast. Then practice the conversation with a partner. Take turns saying each role.

BRIAN: Is everything ready for the presentation tomorrow?

ABBY: Tomorrow? The presentation's on Friday, not tomorrow.

BRIAN: Really? Oh, yes, right. Still, that gives you more time to prepare.

ABBY: Gives me more time? You're giving the presentation, Brian.

BRIAN: Really? Oh, yes, right. Don't worry, I know a lot about Asia. I'll easily finish.

ABBY: Asia? The talk's about our markets in South America and the Middle East!

BRIAN: Really? Oh, yes, right. Well, then, I might need some help.

D Work with a different partner. Choose one of the situations below and make up a conversation that has some examples of contrastive stress. Practice saying your conversation until it feels fluent and natural.

   a. You order some food in a restaurant. The server brings you the wrong dishes.
   b. You call an online store to complain because they sent you the wrong items.

E **RECALL** Think how you would answer these questions using contrastive stress. Then work with a partner. Take turns asking and answering the questions.

   1. Did the women who started Google have a business plan?
   2. Is Do Won Chang's fashion company called Forever 22?
   3. Was Mikaila Ulmer 14 when she started Me & the Bees Lemonade?
   4. Did Qunfei Zhou drop out of college before starting Lens Technology?
   5. Sanga Moses started a rocket fuel company in Egypt, didn't he?
   6. Did Chanda Shroff make clothes to help men from a part of India?

Critical Thinking

F Work in a group. Make questions like the ones in exercise E about Howard Schultz, Anita Roddick, and Yvon Chouinard. Share your questions with another group of students and listen to their responses.

Anita Roddick believed that businesses could be both profitable and ethical.

Review

A **PRONUNCIATION** Underline the words that would have contrastive stress in these sentences. Then practice saying the sentences aloud with natural pronunciation.

1. He doesn't need a little more ambition, confidence, and motivation, he needs a lot more.

2. I respect my brother. He's not very flexible, but he is very fair.

3. I doubt she'll complain more about the problem. I think her aim will be to find a solution.

4. Did they begin working for their new organization last year or was it last month?

B **VOCABULARY** Circle the words in exercise A that you learned in this unit. Then write sentences with those words.

C **GRAMMAR** Write sentences about yourself or people you know using the adverbs of degree in the box. Use each adverb only once.

especially	not really	not very	particularly	very

> *My sister is a very successful businesswoman.*

D **SPEAKING SKILL** Work in a group. Take turns paraphrasing each other's sentences from exercise C.

> *Antonia's sister is really good at business.*

RE-ASSESS What skills or language still need improvement?

OPTION 1 Discuss different kinds of success

A Work in a group. Look at the photo. Discuss what kind of success you think the young woman has achieved and some steps she probably took in order to be successful.

B With a partner, choose THREE types of success below or your own ideas. For each one, discuss what each type of success involves and how you could judge whether a person has achieved it.

- Academic success
- Career success
- Family success
- Financial success
- Personal success
- Athletic success

C With your partner, join another pair of students. Share and discuss your ideas from exercise B.

▼ A student walks to the stage to collect her award during the International Science and Engineering Fair held in the United States.

OPTION 2 Describe a failure that became a success

See Unit 10 Rubric in the Appendix.

A **MODEL** Listen to someone describe a situation that seemed like a failure but actually led to success. Complete the chart. 🔊

Who experienced a failure and what was it?	The speaker's ¹_____, Su. She failed a ²_____ to enter a local high school.
How and why did the failure lead to success?	Su's failure was a ³_____ because she had never failed before. She was upset at first but then changed her ⁴_____. Su realized she had failed because she didn't try hard. She began working hard and got into a great ⁵_____. Because of Su's failure, the speaker improved his ⁶_____ and confidence.

PRESENTATION SKILL Organize Your Talk

In general, talks that are well-organized are easier to understand and easier to deliver. The best organization for a talk will depend on the type of talk and the topic. Some common and effective ways to organize talks include:

- Discussing events in the order they happened
- Describing problems and then their solutions
- Talking about the pros and cons of something
- Explaining the causes and effects of something

B **ANALYZE THE MODEL** Listen again. How does the speaker organize his talk? 🔊

a. He first explains how his talk will be organized. Then he describes a failure that ended up as a success. Finally, he mentions how people reacted.
b. He first gives some background information. Then he describes how somebody failed. Lastly, he explains how this failure led to success.
c. He first introduces his topic in detail. Then he describes the organization of his talk. After that, he discusses a failure that became a success.

C **PLAN** Complete the steps.

1. Decide which failure that became a success you will discuss. This could be an example that you research or one that you already know about.
2. Make notes about what you will say and decide how you will organize your talk.

D **PRACTICE AND PRESENT** Practice giving your presentation with a partner before you present it to the class.

Appendix

I. SPEAKING PHRASES

Giving an Opinion
I think . . .
I believe . . .
In my opinion/view . . .
If you ask me, . . .
Personally, . . .

Asking for an Opinion
What do you think?
What's your opinion?
What are your thoughts?
How do you feel about . . . ?
Do you have anything to add?

Showing Interest
Really?
Wow!
That's funny / interesting / incredible / awful!
Seriously?
No kidding!

Giving a Tip or Suggestion
You/We should/could/shouldn't . . .
I suggest (that) . . .
Let's . . .
How about . . . + (noun/gerund)
Why don't we/you . . .

Agreeing   **Disagreeing**
I agree.   *I disagree.*
Right!   *I'm not sure about that.*
Good point.   *I don't agree.*
Exactly.   *That's a good point, but I disagree.*
Absolutely.

Asking for Repetition
I'm sorry?
Excuse me?
Could you repeat that?
Could you say that again?
Sorry, I didn't catch that.
Sorry, I missed that.

Clarifying
What do you mean?
What does that mean?
Do you mean . . . ?
Could you explain that?
I'm not sure I understand.
I'm not sure what you mean.

Checking Others' Understanding
Do you understand?
Is that clear?
Are you following me?
Do you have any questions?

Rephrasing
In other words, . . .
To put it another way, . . .
What I mean to say . . .
The point I'm making is . . .

Interrupting
Excuse me. / Pardon me.
I'm sorry to interrupt . . .
Can I stop you for a second?
I'd like to add something.

Taking Turns
Can/May I say something?
Could I add something?
May I continue?
Let me finish, please.

Supporting / Praising Others
That's a great/excellent idea.
You make a great point.
Well done.
That's fantastic.

Introducing a Topic
I'm/We're going to talk about . . .
My topic is . . .
I'm/We're going to present . . .
I plan to discuss . . .
Let's start with . . .

Listing or Sequencing
There are many types/kinds of/ways, . . .
First/First of all/The first point, idea/To start/To begin, . . .
Second/Secondly/The second point . . .
Next/Another/Also/Then/In addition, . . .
Last/Finally/The last point . . .

Giving an Example	Repeating and Rephrasing
The first example is . . .	*What you need to know is . . .*
For instance, . . .	*I'll say this again . . .*
For example, . . .	*So again, let me repeat . . .*
. . . such as . . .	*The most important point is . . .*
. . . like . . .	
Defining	**Talking about a Visual**
. . . , which means . . .	*This graph/infographic/diagram shows/explains . . .*
What that means is	*The line/box/image represents . . .*
In other words, . . .	*The main point of this visual is . . .*
Another way to say that is	*From this we can see . . .*
That is . . .	
Concluding	**Participating in a Meeting**
To sum up,	*Welcome, everyone. The purpose of today's meeting is . . .*
In conclusion,	*Today's meeting is to discuss . . .*
In summary,	*Let's move on to the next item.*
	Let me share my screen. Can I share my screen?
	Can you see my screen?
	You can post your questions in the chat box.

II. PRONUNCIATION GUIDE

Vowel and Consonant Symbols

Vowel Sounds

Key Word	Symbol
1. **e**at, d**ee**p	/iʸ/
2. **i**t, d**i**p	/ɪ/
3. l**a**te, p**ai**n	/eʸ/
4. l**e**t, p**e**n	/ɛ/
5. c**a**t, f**a**n	/æ/
6. b**ir**d, t**ur**n	/ɜr/
7. c**u**p, s**u**ffer*	/ʌ/
about, symb**o**l	/ə/
8. h**o**t, st**o**p	/ɑ/
9. t**oo**, n**ew**	/uʷ/
10. g**oo**d, c**ou**ld	/ʊ/
11. r**oa**d, n**o**te	/oʷ/
12. l**aw**, w**a**lk	/ɔ/
13. f**i**ne, r**i**ce	/aʸ/
14. **ou**t, n**ow**	/aʷ/
15. b**oy**, j**oi**n	/ɔʸ/

Consonant Sounds

Key Word	Symbol	Key Word	Symbol
1. **p**ie	/p/	13. **sh**oe	/ʃ/
2. **b**oy	/b/	14. mea**s**ure	/ʒ/
3. **t**en	/t/	15. **ch**oose	/tʃ/
4. **d**ay	/d/	16. **j**ob	/dʒ/
5. **k**ey	/k/	17. **m**y	/m/
6. **g**o	/g/	18. **n**o	/n/
7. **f**ine	/f/	19. si**ng**	/ŋ/
8. **v**an	/v/	20. **l**et	/l/
9. **th**ink	/θ/	21. **r**ed	/r/
10. **th**ey	/ð/	22. **w**e	/w/
11. **s**ee	/s/	23. **y**es	/y/
12. **z**oo	/z/	24. **h**ome	/h/

*The vowel sound/symbol in *cup* and *suffer* is used in stressed words and syllables; the vowel sound/symbol in *about* and *symbol* is used in unstressed syllables.

Source: *Well Said: Pronunciation for Clear Communication*, Fourth Edition, National Geographic Learning/Cengage Learning, 2017.

III. GRAMMAR/VOCABULARY REFERENCES

Irregular Verbs and Past Participles		
Base Verb	Simple Past Verb	Past Participle
become	became	become
begin	began	begun
bet	bet	bet
bite	bit	bitten
break	broke	broken
bring	brought	brought
build	built	built
buy	bought	bought
choose	chose	chosen
come	came	come
cost	cost	cost
cut	cut	cut
dig	dug	dug
draw	drew	drawn
drink	drank	drunk
drive	drove	driven
eat	ate	eaten
fall	fell	fallen
feed	fed	fed
feel	felt	felt
fight	fought	fought
find	found	found
fly	flew	flown
forget	forgot	forgotten
forgive	forgave	forgiven
freeze	froze	frozen
get	got	gotten
give	gave	given
go	went	gone
grow	grew	grown
hear	heard	heard
hide	hid	hidden
hit	hit	hit
hold	held	held
hurt	hurt	hurt
keep	kept	kept

Irregular Verbs and Past Participles		
Base Verb	Simple Past Verb	Past Participle
know	knew	known
lead	led	led
leave	left	left
lend	lent	lent
let	let	let
lose	lost	lost
make	made	made
mean	meant	meant
meet	met	met
pay	paid	paid
put	put	put
quit	quit	quit
read	read	read
ride	rode	ridden
run	ran	run
say	said	said
see	saw	seen
sell	sold	sold
send	sent	sent
set	set	set
sing	sang	sung
sit	sat	sat
sleep	slept	slept
speak	spoke	spoken
spend	spent	spent
stand	stood	stood
swim	swam	swum
take	took	taken
teach	taught	taught
tell	told	told
think	thought	thought
understand	understood	understood
wake	woke	woken
wear	wore	worn
win	won	won
write	wrote	written

Signal Words with the Present Perfect

Examples	Explanation
We **have lived** here **for one year**.	We use *for* + an amount of time: *for two weeks/years, for a while, for a short/long time,* etc.
We **have lived** here **since last year**.	We use *since* with a date, month, year, etc. to show when the action began.
I **have already eaten** dinner, but I **haven't had** dessert **yet**. My friend **has never enjoyed** flying, but I **have always liked** it.	We can use adverbs with the present perfect to say when something has or has not happened. The adverb can come between has/have and the past participle. *Already* can also come after the verb phrase.
We **have traveled** to five countries together **so far**, and we **haven't had** a bad experience **up to now**.	We can use *so far* and *up to now* to show that something repeatedly has or has not happened including in the present moment.
Have you **ever lived** in another country?	We use *ever* in questions with the present perfect to ask if something has happened at any time in the past.

Relative Pronouns as Subjects

> subject
>
> I found a website. **The website** lists my high school classmates.
>
> I found a website **that / which** lists my high school classmates.
>
> ---
>
> Women . . . . sometimes change their last names.
>
> subject
>
> **Women get married.**
>
> Women **who / that** get married sometimes change their last names.

Relative Pronouns as Objects

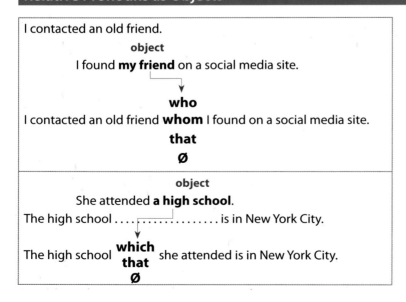

> I contacted an old friend.
>
> object
>
> I found **my friend** on a social media site.
>
> **who**
> I contacted an old friend **whom** I found on a social media site.
> **that**
> **Ø**
>
> ---
>
> object
>
> She attended **a high school**.
>
> The high school . . . . is in New York City.
>
> The high school **which / that / Ø** she attended is in New York City.

Forms of the Passive Voice

	Active	Passive
Simple Present	People **waste** food every day.	Food **is wasted** every day.
Future	Millions **will see** the movie.	The movie **will be seen** by millions
Simple Past	The city **closed** the restaurant.	The restaurant **was closed**.
Present Perfect	The professor **has read** our papers.	Our papers **have been read**.
Infinitive	Someone **has to clean** the house.	The house **has to be cleaned**.
Modal	They **should put** a light here.	A light **should be put** here.

Verbs Followed by Gerunds or Infinitives

Verbs Followed by Gerunds		Verbs Followed by Gerunds or Infinitives		Verbs Followed by Infinitives	
appreciate	mention	begin	need*	agree	offer
avoid	mind	can't stand	prefer	appear	plan
can't help	miss	continue	remember*	ask	pretend
consider	practice	forget*	can(not) stand	choose	promise
discuss	quit	hate	start	claim	refuse
dislike	recommend	like	stop*	decide	seem
enjoy	regret	love	try*	demand	tend
finish	suggest			expect	try
imagine	understand			hope	want
keep				learn	

*The meaning changes between use of gerund and infinitive.
He stopped eating. (He is not eating now.)
He stopped to eat. (He stopped doing something in order to eat.)

Irregular Comparatives and Superlatives

Adjective	Comparative	Superlative
good	better	best
bad	worse	worst
little	less	least
much	more	most
far	further/farther	furthest/farthest

Vocabulary Notebook Template

A vocabulary notebook is a way to keep track of the words you are learning. There are many ways to organize a vocabulary notebook. Here is one way:

Word & part of speech	Definition or synonyms	Antonyms	Example sentence
unique (adj)	unlike anything else; special	common, ordinary	My name is unique; I don't know anyone else who has it.

You many also want to include a translation, other word forms, collocations, etc.
Note what's helpful for you to remember the words.

IV. VOCABULARY INDEX

AW = Academic word

V. SPEAKING RUBRICS

Unit 1: HEALTHY LIVES	Discuss your healthy habits	4	3	2	1
Student name: **Date:** Use this rubric to assess each student's speaking. You can add other aspects of their speaking you'd like to assess at the bottom of the rubric or use the space for more explanation. 4 = Excellent 3 = Good 2 = Satisfactory 1 = Needs improvement	**Content and Organization** • Describes healthy habits well. • Gives clear examples of why the habits are healthy. • Offers ideas and keeps the discussion going.				
	Language Use and Fluency • Uses correct sentence structure, and language is easy to understand and follow. • Uses a variety of words, including phrases for participating in a group discussion, as well as other words taught in the unit. • Speaks smoothly with few hesitations or breaks.				
	Body Language and Voice • Makes good eye contact and uses natural gestures. • Speaks loudly enough for everyone to hear. • Speaks at an appropriate pace.				

Unit 2: TECHNOLOGY TODAY AND TOMORROW	Present a useful app	4	3	2	1
Student name: **Date:** Use this rubric to assess each student's speaking. You can add other aspects of their speaking you'd like to assess at the bottom of the rubric, or use the space for more explanation. 4 = Excellent 3 = Good 2 = Satisfactory 1 = Needs improvement	**Content and Organization** • Recommends an app to classmates. • Says the name of the app and why it's useful. • Gives reasons to support why the app is useful. • Organizes ideas clearly.				
	Language Use and Fluency • Uses correct sentence structure, and language is easy to understand and follow. • Uses a variety of words, including words to introduce reasons, as well as other words taught in the unit. • Speaks smoothly with few hesitations or breaks.				
	Body Language and Voice • Makes good eye contact and uses natural gestures. • Speaks loudly enough for everyone to hear. • Speaks at an appropriate pace.				

Unit 3: CULTURE AND IDENTITY

Student name:

Date:

Use this rubric to assess each student's speaking. You can add other aspects of their speaking you'd like to assess at the bottom of the rubric, or use the space for more explanation.

4 = Excellent
3 = Good
2 = Satisfactory
1 = Needs improvement

Present your identity	4	3	2	1
Content and Organization • Says how other people view them. • Says how they view themselves. • Repeats and emphasizes important words. • Defines unfamiliar terms if necessary. • Organizes ideas clearly.				
Language Use and Fluency • Uses correct sentence structure, and language is easy to understand and follow. • Uses a variety of words, including words taught in the unit. • Speaks smoothly with few hesitations or breaks.				
Body Language and Voice • Makes good eye contact and uses natural gestures. • Speaks loudly enough for everyone to hear. • Speaks at an appropriate pace.				

Unit 4: LET'S EAT

Student name:

Date:

Use this rubric to assess each student's speaking. You can add other aspects of their speaking you'd like to assess at the bottom of the rubric, or use the space for more explanation.

4 = Excellent
3 = Good
2 = Satisfactory
1 = Needs improvement

Debate whether cooking should be taught in schools	4	3	2	1
Content and Organization • Presents reasons to support an opinion. • Supports reasons with details and examples. • Explains why the other team's ideas were less convincing. • Defines unfamiliar terms if necessary. • Organizes ideas clearly.				
Language Use and Fluency • Uses correct sentence structure, and language is easy to understand and follow. • Uses a variety of words, including words to give and ask for opinions, as well as other words taught in the unit. • Speaks smoothly with few hesitations or breaks.				
Body Language and Voice • Makes good eye contact and uses natural gestures. • Speaks loudly enough for everyone to hear. • Speaks at an appropriate pace.				

Unit 5: INSIDE THE BRAIN

Student name:

Date:

Use this rubric to assess each student's speaking. You can add other aspects of their speaking you'd like to assess at the bottom of the rubric, or use the space for more explanation.

4 = Excellent
3 = Good
2 = Satisfactory
1 = Needs improvement

Present advice to future students	4	3	2	1
Content and Organization • Presents a meme that gives advice to future students. • Describes the image and text in the meme. • Explains how the advice relates to learning. • Organizes ideas clearly.				
Language Use and Fluency • Uses correct sentence structure, and language is easy to understand and follow. • Uses a variety of words, including words taught in the unit. • Speaks smoothly with few hesitations or breaks.				
Body Language and Voice • Makes good eye contact and uses natural gestures. • Speaks loudly enough for everyone to hear. • Speaks at an appropriate pace.				

Unit 6: KNOWLEDGE IS POWER

Student name:

Date:

Use this rubric to assess each student's speaking. You can add other aspects of their speaking you'd like to assess at the bottom of the rubric, or use the space for more explanation.

4 = Excellent
3 = Good
2 = Satisfactory
1 = Needs improvement

Present on something you want to study	4	3	2	1
Content and Organization • Says what they want to study and why. • Explains how they will evaluate their learning. • Checks the audience's understanding. • Organizes ideas clearly.				
Language Use and Fluency • Uses correct sentence structure, and language is easy to understand and follow. • Uses a variety of words, including words taught in the unit. • Speaks smoothly with few hesitations or breaks.				
Body Language and Voice • Makes good eye contact and uses natural gestures. • Speaks loudly enough for everyone to hear. • Speaks at an appropriate pace.				

Unit 7: OUR CHANGING WORLD

Student name:

Date:

Use this rubric to assess each student's speaking. You can add other aspects of their speaking you'd like to assess at the bottom of the rubric, or use the space for more explanation.

4 = Excellent
3 = Good
2 = Satisfactory
1 = Needs improvement

Talk about a change in our world	4	3	2	1
Content and Organization • Presents an environmental change and its effects. • Describes how their community or others are responding to the change. • Allows time for each partner to present. • Organizes ideas clearly.				
Language Use and Fluency • Uses correct sentence structure, and language is easy to understand and follow. • Uses a variety of words, including linking words, and other words taught in the unit. • Speaks smoothly with few hesitations or breaks.				
Body Language and Voice • Makes good eye contact and uses natural gestures. • Speaks loudly enough for everyone to hear. • Speaks at an appropriate pace.				

Unit 8: LIVING HISTORY

Student name:

Date:

Use this rubric to assess each student's speaking. You can add other aspects of their speaking you'd like to assess at the bottom of the rubric, or use the space for more explanation.

4 = Excellent
3 = Good
2 = Satisfactory
1 = Needs improvement

Present a historical object, site, or person	4	3	2	1
Content and Organization • Presents a historical object, site, or person. • Says why this topic is important to study today. • Summarizes important facts and details. • Includes information that answers questions the audience may have. • Organizes ideas clearly.				
Language Use and Fluency • Uses correct sentence structure, and language is easy to understand and follow. • Uses a variety of words, including words taught in the unit. • Speaks smoothly with few hesitations or breaks.				
Body Language and Voice • Makes good eye contact and uses natural gestures. • Speaks loudly enough for everyone to hear. • Speaks at an appropriate pace.				

Unit 9: SPECIES SURVIVAL

Student name:

Date:

Use this rubric to assess each student's speaking. You can add other aspects of their speaking you'd like to assess at the bottom of the rubric, or use the space for more explanation.

4 = Excellent
3 = Good
2 = Satisfactory
1 = Needs improvement

Present on an endangered species	4	3	2	1
Content and Organization • Presents an endangered animal. • Says why the animal is endangered. • Suggests ways the community could take action to protect the animal. • Allows an equal amount of time for each partner to present. • Organizes ideas clearly.				
Language Use and Fluency • Uses correct sentence structure, and language is easy to understand and follow. • Uses a variety of words, including words to express causes and effects, and other words taught in the unit. • Speaks smoothly with few hesitations or breaks.				
Body Language and Voice • Makes good eye contact and uses natural gestures. • Speaks loudly enough for everyone to hear. • Speaks at an appropriate pace.				

Unit 10: FINDING SUCCESS

Student name:

Date:

Use this rubric to assess each student's speaking. You can add other aspects of their speaking you'd like to assess at the bottom of the rubric, or use the space for more explanation.

4 = Excellent
3 = Good
2 = Satisfactory
1 = Needs improvement

Describe a failure that became a success	4	3	2	1
Content and Organization • Describes a failure that became a success. • Organizes the talk effectively.				
Language Use and Fluency • Uses correct sentence structure, and language is easy to understand and follow. • Uses a variety of words, including words taught in the unit. • Speaks smoothly with few hesitations or breaks.				
Body Language and Voice • Makes good eye contact and uses natural gestures. • Speaks loudly enough for everyone to hear. • Speaks at an appropriate pace.				

ACKNOWLEDGMENTS

The Authors and Publisher would like to acknowledge the educators around the world who participated in the development of the third edition of *Pathways Listening, Speaking, and Critical Thinking*.

A special thanks to our Advisory Board for their valuable input during development.

Advisory Board

Baher F. AlDabba, Amideast Gaza; **Hossein Askari**, Houston Community College; **Dilara Ataman Akalin**, TOBB University; **Andrew Boon**, Toyo Gakuen University; **Fatih Bozoğlu**, Antalya Bilim University; **Julie Cote**, Houston Community College; **Kristen Cox**, Global Launch at ASU; **Patricia Fiene**, Midwestern Career College; **Ronnie Hill**, Royal Melbourne Institute of Technology; **Greg Holloway**, University of Kitakyushu; **Ragette Jawad**, Lawrence Technological University; **Elizabeth Macdonald**, Sacred Heart University; **Daniel Paller**, Kinjo Gakuin University; **Kes Poupaert**, INTO Manchester; **Juan Quintana**, Instituto Cultural Peruano Norteamericano; **Anouchka Rachelson**, Miami Dade College; **David Ruzicka**, Shinsu University; **Gabrielle Smallbone**, Kingston University; **Debra Wainscott**, Baylor University

Global Reviewers

Asia

John Paul Abellera, San Beda College-Alabang; **Andrew Acosta**, Udonpittayanukoon School; **Jherwin Adora**, Department of Education Philippines; **Mubarak Ali**, Unilever; **Joan Arado**, TESDA PTS-Misamis Occidental; **Frederick Bacala**, Yokohama City University; **Katherine Bauer**, Clark Memorial International High School; **Richard Bent**, Kwassui Women's University; **Teresa Bolen**, Ryukoku University; **Johnny Burns**, Kansai Daigaku; **Darine Chehwan**, Rest-art Studio; **Simon Cornelius**, Kansai University; **Aurelio Da Costa**, UNICEF/Senai Language Centre; **Carlos Daley**, London Institute; **Maria del Vecchio**, Nihon University; **Ria De Ocera**, Udomsuksa School; **Michael Donzella**, Kaichi International University; **David Groff**, Meiji University; **Akiko Hagiwara**, Tokyo University of Pharmacy and Life Sciences; **Sisilia Halimi**, Humanities Universitas Indonesia; **Jane Harland**, Fukoka University; **Makoto Hayashi**, Nagoya University; **Patrizia Hayashi**, Meikai University; **Andrea Noemie Hilomen**, Private teacher; **Ha Hoang**, Au Chau Language School; **Ana Sofia Hofmeyr**, Kansai University; **Stephen Hofstee**, Kanto Gakuin University; **Stephen Howes**, Tokyo Seitoku University Fukaya Junior High School; **Yuko Igarashi**, Ritsumeikan University; **Mari Inoue**, Tokyo University of Science; **David Johnson**, Kyushu Sangyo University; **Sarita Joyaka**, Nongkipittayakhom; **Chong Jui Jong**, Universiti Sains Malaysia; **Yuko Kawae**, Kindai University; **Megumi Kobayashi**, Seikei University; **Mutsumi Kondo**, Kyoto University of Foreign Studies; **Gomer Jay Legaspi**, Caraga State University; **Indah Ludij**, Academic Writing Center, Universitas Indonesia; **Kelly MacDonald**, Fukuoka University; **Anh Mai**, Van Lang University; **Tiina Matikainen**, Tamagawa University; **Eiko Matsubara**, Rissho University; **Jason May**, Den-en Chofu Gakuen; **Sean Collin Mehmet**, Matsumoto University; **Mabell Mingoy**, Teach for the Philippines; **Mari Miyao**, Kyoto University of Foreign Studies; **Wah Mon**, Private teacher; **Masaki Mori**, Aoyama-Gakuinn University; **Gerald Muirhead**, Tohoku Gakuin University; **Charlotte Murakami**, Kurume University; **Duong Nguyen**, APU; **Ly Huyền Nguyễn**, FPT High School; **Vinh Nguyen**, Hanoi University; **Ngan Nguyễn**; **Thảo Nguyễn**, Gia Việt English Center; **MaiKhoi NguyenThi**, Danang Architecture University; **Takeshi Nozawa**, Ritsumeikan University; **Naomi Ogasawara**, Gunma Prefectural Women's University; **Mari Ogawa**, Meiji University; **Megumi Okano**, Keio University; **Hisako Osuga**, Meiji University; **Gellian Ostrea**, Manolo Fortich National High School; **Tina Ottman**, Doshisha University, Bukkyo University; **Ardy Paembonan**, SMA El-Shaddai Jayapura; **Anthony Paxton**, Ibaraki Prefectural Takezono High School; **Hong Pham**, Brendon Primary School; **Huong Pham**, Foreign Languages Specialised School, University of Languages and International Studies; **John Plagens** Lutheran College; **Javeria Rana**, The City School; **Rebecca Reyes**, Captain Albert Aguilar National High School; **Florencio Salmasan**, School of the Holy Spirit; **Sherri Scanlan**, Toyama Prefectural University; **Naoki Senrui**, Komazawa University; **Nanik Shobikah**, IAIN Pontianak; **Coleman South**, Saga National University; **Yukiko Sugiyama**, Keio University; **Pavloska Susanna**, Doshisha University; **Eri Tamura**, Ishikawa Prefectural University; **Yuko Tokisato**, Kansai University; **Saeko Toyoshima**, Tsuru University; **Janssen Undag**, Darunapolytechnic Technological College; **Carl Vollmer**, Ritsumeikan Uji Junior and Senior High School; **Isra Wongsarnpigoon**, Kanda University of International Studies

Europe

Ana Maria Andrei, Liceul Teoretic de Informatica; **Regina Bacanskiene**, Kaunas School; **Janice Bain**, Glasgow International College; **Oana Banu**, LPS; **Daniela Berntzen**; **Sarah Bishopp**, Kaplan International College London; **Anna Broumerioti**; **Cath Brown**, The University of Sheffield; **Laura Cannella**, Kaplan International College London; **Barbara Cavicchiolli**, INTO Manchester; **Ioana Mirela Cojocaru**, Liceul Tehnologic Anghel Saligny; **Viorica Condrat**, USARB; **Astrid D'Andrea**, I.I.S. Croce-Aleramo; **Liesl Daries**, English with Liesl; **Kurtis De Souza-Snares**, Kaplan International Pathways; **Elona Dhepa**, 7 Marsi; **Maral Dosmagambetova**, Lingua College; **Camelia-Adriana Dulau**, Simion Bărnuțiu; **Ruthanna Farragher**, Kaplan; **Olesia Fesenko**, Vyshhorod Lyceum "Suziria"; **Cristina Foltmann**, ITCS Abba Ballini; **Laura Gheorghita**, Scoala Gimnaziala Grigore Geamanu Turcinesti; **Marian Gonzalez**, Liceo de Idiomas Modernos; **Paulina Holesz**, Private teacher; **Lindsey Hollywood**, Universtiy of Liverpool International College; **Sarah Hopwood**, University of Nottingham International College; **Barbara Howarth**, Glasgow International College; **Barbara Howarth**, Glasgow International College; **Jana Jilkova**, ICV & Pedagogical Faculty; **Alina Loata**, Colegiul National Dimitrie Cantemir; **Ia Manjgaladze**, Access Program Teacher; **Christiana Mili**, Private teacher; **Laura Morrison**,

Glasgow International College; **Robert Pinkham-Smith**, University of Essex International College; **Yuliya Pokroyeva**, Private teacher; **Eva Rodaki**, Private teacher; **Alina Rotaru**, Twinkle Star; **Carme RR**, CEIP Joan Mas Pollença; **Tatiana Silvesan**, Centrul Scolar de Educatie Incluziva; **Bianca Somesan**, Palatul Copiilor Targu Mures; **Elena Strugaru**, Britanica Learning Centre; **Mina Vermot**, Miduca; **Matthew Wilson**, Brunel University London; **Emily Wright**, Arden University

Latin America and the Caribbean

Maria Aguilar, Universidad Nacional de La Rioja; **Karina Aldana**, Colegio la Asuncion; **Mariela Amarante**, Sunshine Academy; **Auricéa Bacelar**, Top Seven Idiomas; **Verónica Bonilla**, Universidad Anáhuac de Puebla; **Lucila Caballero**, MEDUCA; **Milagros Calderón Miró**, Colegio San Antonio IHM; **Maria Carrizo**, Nores; **Erika Ceballos**, Escuela Nacional Preparatoria; **Johana Coronel**, Private teacher; **Marcelo D'Elia**, Centro Britanico Idiomas; **Sophia De Carvalho**, Inglês Express; **Corina Diaz**, CCSA; **Isabela Dias**, Inglês Express; **Joseph Duque**, Unidad Educativa Leibnitz; **Esperanza Espejo**, Iteso; **Susana Espinosa**, ICPNA; **Carolina Ferreira**, Private teacher; **Matheus Figueiredo**, Private teacher; **Andrea Garcia Hernandez**, Bilingual School; **Alessandra Gotardo**, IYEnglish - Language & Culture; **Santo Guzmán**, JFK Institute of Languages, inc.; **Cecibel Juliao**, Meduca / Udelas; **Letícia Kayano**, Private teacher; **Sandra Landi**, Private teacher; **Patricia Lanners**, Universidad de las Americas Puebla; **Arenas Laura**, ITESO; **Diana Lopez**, ITSE; **Mario López Ayala**, Universidad Autónoma de Sinaloa; **Rosa Awilda Lopez Fernandez**, Universidad Acción Pro-Educación y Culturalic Dominicana; **Fabricio Romeo Mejia Lopez**, Academia Europea; **Silvia Luna**, Universidad Evangélica; **Manuel Malhaber Diaz**, Colegio Nacional San Juan De Chota; **Daniel Martins Aragão**, Private teacher; **Victor Hugo Medina Soares**, Cultura Inglesa Belo Horizonte; **Angélica Parada**, CBA; **Adela Perez del Viso**, Fundación E.S.Y.C.; **Byron Quinde**, Unidad Educativa Particular de la Asunción; **Maria Alejandra Quirch**, Instituto San Roman; **Joselyn Ramos Cuba**, UNMSM; **Jorge Reategui**, Universidad Continental; **Jazmin Reyes**, La Dolorosa; **Iliana Rivas**, ITESO; **Sheirys Hidalgo Ruiz**, Ministerio de Educacion Publica; **Adelina Ruiz Guerrero**, Instituto Tecnológico y de Estudios Superiores de Occidente; **Maribel Santiago**, Colegio de Bachilleres; **Margaret Simons**, English Center; **Margaret Simons**, English Center; **Sheily Sosa García**, ICPNA; **Jane Stories**, Private teacher; **María Trigos**, ITSX; **Henrique Ucci**, Liverpool English Institute; **Ana Carolina Vargas Arreola**, Colegio Vizcaya; **Laura Zurutuza**, ITESO

Middle East and Africa

Merve Akyiğit, Adana Doğa Schools; **Yousef Albozom**, America-Mideast Educational and Training Services; **Rehab Alzeiny**, IPS; **Rais Attamimi**, UTAS-Salalah; **Ezgi Avar**, Tuzla Doğa Lisesi; **Pınar Çakır**, Doğa Koleji; **Burçe Çimeli**, Doğa Koleji; **Christelle Gernique Djoukouo Talla**, Government Bilingual High School Ekangte; **Canan Dülger**, Doğa Koleji; **Manal ElMazbouh**, American University of the Middle East; **Fatma el-zahraa El-sayed zaki nassef**, Damietta Official Language schools; **Necmi Ersungur**, İtü Eta Vakfı Doğa Koleji; **Mary Goveas**, University of Bahrain; **Farhad Hama**, Sulaimani University; **Michael King**, Community College of Qatar; **Georgios Kormpas**, Al Yamamah University; **Volga Kurbanzade**, Okan University; **Eni Ermawati Lasito**, Lusail University; **Gonca Mavuk**, Atasehir ITU Doga College; **Amina Moubtassim**, ALC; **Doaa Najjar**, PISOD; **Mohammad Esmaeel Nasrabadi**, Private teacher; **Naki Erhan Ozer**, Doga Schools; **Rehab Raouf**, Al Safwa School; **Nurhayat Şenman**, Özlüce Doğa Koleji Lise; **Choukri Serhane**, CHSS; **Hussam Tannera**, America-Mideast Educational and Training Services; **Pedro Vemba**, Liceu do Soyo; **Cüneyt Yüce**, Istanbul Okan University

USA and Canada

Galyna, Arabadzhy, St. Cloud State University; **Elizabeth Armstrong**, Midwestern Career College; **Judy Bagg**, Pierce; **Karin Bates**, Intercambio Uniting Communities; **Mandie Bauer**, ASC English; **Elisabeth Bowman**, Schoolcraft College; **Teresa Cheung**, North Shore Community College; **Colleen Comidy**, Seattle Central College; **Jacquelin Cunningham**, Harold Washington College; **Jean Danic**, Hillsborough Community College; **Rosalia dela Cruz**, NorQuest College; **Christine Dick**, Arizona State University; **Yvonne Dunham Slobodenko**, University of Tennessee at Chattanooga; **Karen Eichhorn**, International English Center; **Thomas Fox**, Dallas College; **Diana Garcia**, Union County College; **Bertha George**, Union County College; **Thomas Germain**, University of Colorado Boulder; **Debra Gibes**, Mott Community College; **John Glover**, Old Saybrook High School; **Christine Guro**, University of Hawaii at Manoa; **Carrie Hein-Paredes**, MATC; **Deanna Henderson**, Language Consultants International; **Tom Justice**, North Shore Community College; **Evan Kendall**, Los Angeles City College; **Michael Kelley**, Hillsborough Community College; **Karen E. Kyle**, Aims Community College; **Laura Lamour**, Florida International University; **Maureen Lanseur**, Henry Ford College; **Heidi Lieb**, Bergen Community College; **Layla Malander**, PLACE/Colorado State University; **Tim Mathews**, Nashville State Community College; **Richard McDorman**, Language On; **Susan McElwain**, Mohawk College of Applied Arts and Technology; **Jason McKenzie**, Apex Language and Career College; **William Miller Jr.**, H.EN; **Lilia Myers Van Pelt**, Colorado State University Pueblo; **Sandra Navarro**, Glendale Community College; **Linda Neuman**, Anne Arundel Community College; **Susan Niemeyer**, Los Angeles City College; **Mariah Nix**, Lumos Language School; **Cheryl Pakos**, Union County College; **Jim Papple**, York University; **Cora Perrone**, Southern CT State University; **Deborah Pfeifer**, Fort Hays State University; **Loretta Quan**, Schoolcraft College; **Thomas Riedmiller**, University of Northern; **Lisa Rivoallon**, Gavilan College; **Noele Simmons**, George Mason University; **Pamela Smart-Smith**, Virginia Tech; **Kelly Smith**, English Language Institute, UCSD Extension; **Brandt Snook**, University of Louisiana – Lafayette; **Shoshanna Starzynski**, Global Launch, Arizona State University; **Kirsten Stauffer**, Immigrant and Refugee Center of Northern Colorado; **JoAnn Stehly**, North Orange County Community College District; **Karen Vallejo**, University of California, Irvine; **Sharifeh Van Court**, Dallas College; **Melissa Vervinck**, ESL Institute at Oakland University; **Christy Williams**, INTO USF; **Paula Yerman**, Los Angeles City College

CREDITS

Illustrations: All illustrations are owned by © Cengage

Cover ©Craig Cutler/National Geographic Image Collection; **ii** (tl) VCG/Getty Images, (cl1) Philip Fong/AFP/Getty Images, (cl2) © Kiliii Yuyan/National Geographic Image Collection, (cl3) Runner of art/Moment/Getty Images, (bl) © Catherine Panebianco; **iv** (tl) Dado Ruvic/Reuters, (cl1) Daniel J Barr/Moment/Getty Images, (cl2) © Sebastien Nagy, (cl3) Matthew Maran/Nature Picture Library, (bl Gabi Vogt/13 Photo/Redux); **vi** (t) Andriy Onufriyenko/Moment/Getty Images, (c1) Stephen Chung/Alamy Stock Photo, (c2) K-Kucharska_D-Kucharski/iStock/Getty Images; **vii** Regina Tremmel/Anzenberger/Redux; **1** VCG/Visual China Group/Getty Images; **2** Abaca Press/Alamy Stock Photo; **4** Cultura RM Exclusive/Antonio Saba/Getty Images; **7** Ben Birchall - PA Images/Getty Images; **9** AP Images/San Francisco Chronicle/Liz Hafalia; **11** Thomas_EyeDesign/E+/Getty Images; **12** Denis Moura/500px/Getty Images; **15** Science Photo Library/Getty Images; **16–17** (spread) Mlenny/E+/Getty Images; **19** Adamkaz/E+/Getty Images; **21** Philip Fong/AFP/Getty Images; **22** Oscar Wong/Getty Images; **22–23** (spread) Andreas von Einsiedel/Corbis Documentary/Getty Images; **27** Sarah Blesener/The New York Times/Redux Pictures; **31** National Geographic Image Collection; **33** Stephen J. Cohen/Getty Images Entertainment/Getty Images; **35** Jasmin Merdan/Moment/Getty Images; **36** Mondadori Portfolio/Getty Images; **39** Ted Hsu/Alamy Stock Photo; **40** Peter DaSilva/The New York Times/Redux Pictures; **41** © Kiliii Yuyan/National Geographic Image Collection; **42–43** (spread) Giuseppe Cacace/AFP/Getty Images; **44** Jorge Fernández/LightRocket/Getty Images; **47** © Natalie Keyssar; **50** © Marco Vernaschi/National Geographic Image Collection; **51** © Erika Larsen/National Geographic Image Collection; **52** Panther Media GmbH/Alamy Stock Photo; **55** Jessica Nabongo; **57** JohnnyGreig/E+/Getty Images; **59** Xavierarnau/E+/Getty Images; **61** Runner of art/Moment/Getty Images; **62–63** (spread) © Sean McNaughton/5W Infographics/Jason Lee/Rebecca Hale Sources-University of Twente Netherlands andWaterfootprint.org/National Geographic Image Collection; **66–67** (spread) Chris Holdsworth/Shutterstock.com; **70** Ryasick/E+Getty Images; **71** Olga Yastremska/Alamy Stock Photo; **77** Westend61/Getty Images; **79** Maskot/Getty Images; **81** © Catherine Panebianco; **82–83** (spread) Andriy Onufriyenko/Moment/Getty Images; **87** Hugo Hu/Getty Images News/Getty Images; **89** © National Geographic Image Collection; **91** Rick Friedman/Corbis News/Getty Images; **94** © John Burcham/National Geographic Image Collection; **97** © Matt Moyer; **99** Picture Alliance/Getty Images; **101** Dado Ruvic/Reuters; **102** Matt Hazlett/Getty Images Sport/Getty Images; **102–103** (spread) Steve Boye/Sports Illustrated Classic/Getty Images; **104** Cynthia Johnson//Time Life Pictures/Getty Images; **106** Catherine Falls Commercial/Moment/Getty Images; **109** Brian van der Brug/Los Angeles Times/Getty Images; **110** Tempura/E+/Getty Images; **111** Picture alliance/Getty Images; **113** SDI Productions/E+/Getty Images; **115** © Mike Gil; **117** Peter Llewellyn/Alamy Stock Photo; **119** © Ciril Jazbec/National Geographic Image Collection; **121** Daniel J Barr/Moment/Getty Images; **122** © Ciril Jazbec/National Geographic Image Collection; **123** (t) © Alize Carrre, (b) Jonas Bendiksen/Magnum Photos; **124** (bl1) Michal Sikorski/Alamy Stock Photo, (bl2) Mik39/Alamy Stock Photo, (bc) Matthias Kulka/The Image Bank/Getty Images, (br1) Terry Vine/The Image BankGetty Images, (br2) Robert McGouey/Wildlife/Alamy Stock Photo; **126** Philippe Psaila/Science Source; **128** Ryan McGinnis/Moment/Getty Images; **131** Tom Wang/Alamy Stock Photo; **132** Spc3mky/Alamy Stock Photo; **134** Rainer Lesniewski/Alamy Stock Photo; **137** Mario Tama/Getty Images News/Getty Images; **139** Akiyo/iStock/Getty Images; **141** © Sebastien Nagy; **142–143** (spread) The Washington Post/Getty Images; **144** (cl) Bildagentur-online/Universal Images Group/Getty Images, (cr) The Picture Art Collection/Alamy Stock Photo, (bl) Mikroman6/Moment/Getty Images, (br) Artie Photography (Artie Ng)/Moment/Getty Images; **147** Ole Jensen/Getty Images Entertainment/Getty Images; **149** Lubo Ivanko/iStock/Getty Images; **151** Dan Kitwood/Getty Images News/Getty Images; **153** PA Images/Alamy Stock Photo; **155** Tommy Trenchard/Panos Pictures/Redux; **157** Kenneth Garrett/Danita Delimont, Agent/Alamy Stock Photo; **159** Regina Tremmel/Anzenberger/Redux; **161** Matthew Maran/Nature Picture Library; **162** Xinhua News Agency/Getty Images; **162–163** (spread) © Thomas Peschak/National Geographic Image Collection, © Elliot McGucken; **164** Robert Pickett/Corbis Documentary/Getty Images; **166** Stephen Chung/Alamy Stock Photo; **168** Cyril Ruoso/Minden Pictures; **171** K-Kucharska_D-Kucharski/iStock/Getty Images; **173** Scenics & Science/Alamy Stock Photo; **174** Jose A. Bernat Bacete/Moment/Getty Images; **177** © Joel Sartore/National Geographic Image Collection; **179** NurPhoto/Getty Images; **181** Gabi Vogt/13 Photo/Redux; **182–183** (spread) Murray Close/Moviepix/Getty Images; **187** David Strick/Redux; **188** Maskot/Getty Images; **191** © Kat Keene Hogue/National Geographic Image Collection; **192** Santosh Varky/Alamy Stock Photo; **194** © Jeff Johnson/Patagonia; **197** Gavin Smith/Camera Press/Redux; **199** © Dina Litovsky/National Geographic Image Collection.